Future War Novels

Future War Novels:

An Annotated Bibliography of Works in English Published Since 1946

by John Newman and
Michael Unsworth

ORYX PRESS
1984

The rare Arabian Oryx is believed to have inspired the myth of the unicorn. This desert antelope became virtually extinct in the early 1960s. At that time several groups of international conservationists arranged to have 9 animals sent to the Phoenix Zoo to be the nucleus of a captive breeding herd. Today the Oryx population is over 400 and herds have been returned to reserves in Israel, Jordan, and Oman.

Copyright © 1984 by
The Oryx Press
2214 North Central at Encanto
Phoenix, Arizona 85004-1483

Published simultaneously in Canada

Printed and Bound in the United States of America

Library of Congress Cataloging in Publication Data

Newman, John, 1942–
    Future war novels.

    Includes index.
    1. War stories, English—Bibliography.   2. War stories, American—Bibliography.   3. English fiction—20th century —Bibliography.   4. American fiction—20th century— Bibliography.   5. Science fiction, English—Bibliography. 6. Science fiction, American—Bibliography.   7. Future in literature—Bibliography.   8. Atomic warfare in literature —Bibliography.   I. Unsworth, Michael.   II. Title.
    Z2014.F4N43   1984   016.823′080356   83-43245
    [PR888.W37]
    ISBN 0-89774-103-X

Jeu
12-11-87

Contents

Acknowledgements

This bibliography was compiled with much assistance from friends and colleagues at Colorado State University Libraries and at other libraries in this country and abroad. Special thanks for active help are due to Ann Hilfinger, who provided a generous measure of excellent staff support, and to Evan Vlachos, who lent books and ideas to the project.

Introduction

In 1945, the United States presented to the rest of the world what most people regard as convincing evidence that our species had finally acquired the means to utterly destroy itself. Since the atomic bombing of Hiroshima and Nagasaki, several nations have tested nuclear weapons, and others are thought to have built them. Despite many opportunities and suggestions since 1945, no further bombs or other nuclear devices have been used in war. This restraint by those whose hands are on the triggers may be due to their good judgment or to the good luck of us all. However, nuclear war is not unthinkable, as persons outraged at the idea sometimes say. Indeed, we think and write about nuclear war, and future war in general, all of the time. This book is about some of that speculation.

The focus of this bibliography is novels written after 1945, the beginning of the atomic weapons age, and before 1984, the year of Orwell's grim literary speculation. The earliest work found was published in 1946, and the bibliography was compiled in 1983, so some later books from the last year may not have been seen. All of the works included have to do with wars that occur in at least the nominal or immediate future among existing nations on earth or close parallels to them. Many of the novels address future nuclear war or its aftermath. Others deal with nonnuclear or limited wars. It is important to include works in the latter category because all wars fought since 1945, especially those involving major powers, have certainly occurred in the context of nuclear possibilities. The fiction since 1945, even that dealing with small or undeclared wars, reflects a political and military situation in which weapons are never far over the horizon.

The range and conceptual vigor of speculative literature suggest that some further indication of the scope of this work is in order. The emphasis is on realistic novels that focus on military events. That eliminates stories of near-war, nuclear blackmail, future ecological or social disasters caused by something other than war, and stories in which some mention is made of remote or unimportant past wars. To avoid extending the scope of this bibliography into general fields of science fiction in which wars proliferate, the working definition excludes stories of space travel beyond the moon, time travel, imaginary beings, parallel universes, alternative history, and magic. The several exceptions to these general guidelines are noted in the annotations in which they occur.

Those who see future war literature in broader terms may be critical of this narrow scope but some limits are necessary. The novels here relate in a realistic way to general human concerns, at least as they are known in the free world, about nuclear weapons and future war. Other books might have been included, but a reading of the annotations and the novels themselves suggests that even this limited scope provides a sufficiency of horrible ideas.

The chronological arrangement allows each work to be seen in the social, political, and military context of its creation. This arrangement is similar to the pattern established by I.F. Clarke in *Voices Prophesying War* (1966) and other seminal studies of the literature of the future. Within each year, further arrangement is by author, and author and title indexes are provided.

This study is based on the comprehensive collection of Imaginary War Fiction at Colorado State University Libraries. Works not found there were borrowed through interlibrary loan or from friends or were purchased. Every title has been searched through all available print and electronic media for information for the bibliographic descriptions prepared by Michael Unsworth. The standard bibliographic entries are supplemented with the full names of lesser-known publishers, pagination and Library of Congress card numbers (or International Standard Book Numbers* if one is known where an LC number is not) when available, and a listing of as many other English language editions as could be identified. All of this additional information is supplied to facilitate bibliographic searching by persons who may not have a book in hand.

In addition to the bibliographic citation, each entry includes an annotation prepared by John Newman. Every attempt is made to convey the essence of the book fairly and on its own terms. A present or past war is emphasized in each story because that is what they all have in common. The annotations must convey essential information about locale, plot, characterization, and military details in a short space, so they are more often descriptive than evaluative. However, when the literary qualities of an author, be they good or bad, deserve special mention, they receive it. To prepare the annotations, each book was read entirely.

---

*Editor's Note: ISBN numbers are reproduced exactly as found in the bibliographic source material.

1946–1949

1946

1. Jenkins, Will F. *The Murder of the U.S.A.* New York: Crown, 1946. 172 pp, Kingston, NY: Handi-Book Mysteries, 1946 127 pp.

Jenkins's characterizations and dialog are by no means realistic, but his vision of the weapons and tactics of future war is prophetic. Two-thirds of the U.S. population are killed in an unexpected atomic attack from an unknown nation. Bombs are guided over the poles to targets that include military facilities, population centers, and mountain lakes that feed irrigation and drinking water systems. Military survivors in a hardened site in the Rocky Mountains intercept later bombs with proximity-fused antimissiles. Later, they encounter spies with medical implants and identify foreign weapons that embody the results of industrial espionage. As the war extends over several days, the Americans locate the nation that attacked them and wreak terrible vengeance. This novel, published the year after a war in which most participants used bolt-action rifles, accurately predicts the military technology of the 1980s.

2. Karig, Walter. *War in the Atomic Age?* New York: Wise, 1946. 63 pp. In 2076, the U.S. is attacked by Galaxy, an "unnatural alliance of nations that had made itself heir to the Axis Powers." Galaxy first destroys Kansas City with an atomic bomb, then asks the U.S. to surrender. The president refuses, and the war is on. Galaxy utilizes an interesting technical innovation in the form of icebergs converted to launching platforms for atomic weapons. This and other naval aspects of the book are to be expected from Karig, a reserve naval officer. Other innovative and horrible methods of mass destruction include biological warfare, a modern form of Greek fire, alteration of ocean currents, and sonic beams. In the end, American courage and scientific ability triumph, and Galaxy surrenders. The characters are perfunctory, the language suggests juvenile literature, and the illustrations add little. Even so, this short book, written almost 40 years ago, makes startlingly accurate predictions about the directions of weapons research in our time. Karig's message is that future war is serious, and we had better be ready.

1947

3. Eldershaw, M. Barnard. *Tomorrow and Tomorrow*. Melbourne, Australia: Georgian House, 1947. 466 pp.

Every page of this long book is heavy going. Characters think and speak in long paragraphs, and much of what occupies them is trite, repetitive observations about the nature of humankind. The story moves back and forth between the twentieth century and a time some centuries in the future. The future Australians are members of the Tenth Commune, a society that combines elements of egalitarianism and meritocracy. As they dig through the ruins of Sydney for clues to the former civilization, they locate a few relics from which they draw original and sometimes accurate conclusions about the people who made them. The twentieth-century Australians live through the Depression, World War II, and a subsequent war that combines elements of both civil war and invasion. It is during this last war that Sydney is burned. Australian readers might be able to make better sense of this novel because they would be more familiar with the many Australian personalities and national characteristics that seem to dominate the author's thinking.

4. Engel, Leonard, and Piller, Emanuel S. *World Aflame*. New York: Dial Press, 1947. 126 pp.

The authors envision a war between the U.S. and Russia that is notable for its length, its ferocity, and the scientific innovations of its weapons. Unlike many other early books, the U.S. is not the innocent victim of a dastardly surprise attack. In fact, the U.S. begins the war in 1950 by dropping atomic bombs on Russia after a series of incidents and provocations. Russia retaliates, and a five-year war begins which includes not only atomic weapons but also germ warfare against crops and people, guided missiles launched from submarines, and abortive American invasions of Russian territory. Numerous cities around the world are destroyed, and civilian populations suffer terrible losses. In 1953, England elects a Labor government and takes itself out of the war, but America fights on. The book is presented as an interim report by a journalist. The war is still going on in 1955, with no end in sight.

5. Leinster, Murray. *Fight for Life*. New York: Crestwood, 1947. 118 pp.
Like other early novels of atomic war, *Fight for Life* is imaginative and original. At one level, it describes a group of essentially decent people who try to survive a nationwide reversion to savagery in the months after an atomic war. The enemy is not known but is still alive and active, for spies among the bands of looters radio back information about any remaining centers of civilization in the U.S., which are soon bombed. On another level, this fairly routine future war scenario contains an unusual element in the form of magic stones from atomic bomb craters. These are found by the central characters who learn to use them to influence the future by wishing for things to happen. The stone can also alter and create electrical energy. This new form of energy finally enables the Americans to resume the fight against the unknown enemy with a technology that seems to promise victory.

1948

6. Dahl, Roald. *Sometime Never*. New York: Scribner's, 1948. 244 pp.
In this novel, gremlins are small creatures who live beneath the surface of the earth and may be part of the human imagination. Gremlins appear briefly in World War II. Then, they conceal themselves during the utterly destructive World War III, a global conflict that appears to have employed only conventional weapons a few years after the second World War. The remnants of humanity arm themselves with atomic and biological weapons and, within a short time, World War IV destroys all living things except the lowest forms of life, and these creatures inherit the earth. Gremlins are cynical observers of humans and caustic analysts of the human condition. Unfortunately, they disappear without apparent cause, just as the last humans have expired. Mention of weapons much like neutron and suitcase bombs is notable in this early work.

7. Farjeon, J. Jefferson. *Death of a World*. London: Collins, 1948. 192 pp.
Space travelers from another planet appear in this novel, but their role is only to discover the ruined planet earth and the diary of John Smith. It is the latter document that provides the story. Farjeon makes it difficult for his readers to stay interested in his narrative and to learn

his characters. The story emerges in thoughts and conversations that are unusually digressive, tedious, and hard to follow. However, a determined reader can learn that Smith, an English clerk, stumbles onto a shelter complex in Wales that is built to house some 200 persons. Captured by the farsighted inhabitants of the shelter, Smith is forced by them to remain underground while a war rages. A miracle substance, melignite, fails in its intended function to seal the shelter from the devastation outside. Persons who venture from the shelter turn literally to dust, and it seems that the principal weapon employed in the new war is a sort of destructive ray. In the end, inhabitants of the shelter become victims of the innovative weapon, and Smith, the last one alive, records it all until his diary ends abruptly.

1949

8. Balint, Emery. *Don't Inhale It!* New York: Gaer Associates, 1949. 222 pp.

The most notable feature of this work is its humor. It is ironic that a book written so soon after the only use of atomic weapons in human experience is one of the few future war stories that is in any way funny. This one is done in heavy satire that sometimes succeeds. The story supposes that an American atomic bomb test in 1960 blows the planet into two pieces. On both surviving earths, caricatures of many human types, races, political groups, and institutions work out many permutations of the future. Most of the situations are brief, and many are silly. The relentless, self-conscious satire works best in the beginning of the book where the author introduces an original idea with good humorous potential and several promising characters. Later in the book, the quality of characterization declines in favor of repetitious antics of future societies. The author's illustrations contribute nothing.

9. FitzGibbon, Constantine. *The Iron Hoop*. New York: Knopf, 1949. 268 pp. LC 49-10556. Other Edition: London: Cassel, 1950, 268 pp.

FitzGibbon's later book, *When the Kissing Had to Stop* (1973, entry 125), is much better, but this earlier effort shows the same ability to sustain an interesting and complex plot and to invent realistic characters. Unfortunately, both books share a sense that people are caught up in drab events that will end badly. A preface explains that the places and characters are intended to be without specific nationality or time. The setting is an occupied city some 10 years after a conventional modern war. The plot involves a resistance uprising. The characters include a stern but just senior officer, his weak nephew, the nephew's mistress who is also a resistance member, and various patriots. Much of the story is told through conversations among characters, which convey a convincing but boring explanation of why people in their particular circumstances should feel hopeless and depressed.

10. Heinlein, Robert A. *Sixth Column*. New York: Gnome Press, 1949. 256 pp. Other Title: *The Day after Tomorrow*, New York: New American Library, 1951, 160 pp. Other Editions; Toronto, Canada: New American Library of Canada, 1970, 144 pp; London: New English Library, 1972, 1979, 141 pp.

After America is conquered by PanAsians in the near future, a group of American soldiers retreats to the Citadel, a prepared fortress in the Colorado mountains. Using advanced technology stored there, the men devise and adapt superior futuristic weapons to use against the occupying forces. Their special breakthrough is military hardware that can alter the form of matter. They also devise weapons that attack certain racial groups but not others. The soldiers spread a resistance organization under the cover of a religion that is acceptable to the PanAsians. Although the war of liberation is not easy, the Americans are ultimately able to defeat their occupiers.

11. Jameson, Storm. *The Moment of Truth*. New York: Macmillan, 1949. 179 pp.

Conflict between loyalty to a dying government and considerations of personal survival occupy the minds of about 10 characters waiting at a remote airbase in northern England for the last plane to America. The setting is the immediate future, and Europe has been overrun by the Red Army. England awaits the army of occupation while assorted persons—military officers, scientists, women, children, workers, and traitors—consider their individual chances for a seat on the evacuation airplane. Apparently, neither the author nor the characters feel any urgency because there is abundant time for long discussions of many matters that have nothing to do with the desperate situation. The dialog would be realistic if it were set in a country house during a fox hunting weekend, but it is too relaxed for persons who are working out which of them will live and which will die. When the airplane comes and choices are made or imposed, characters act according to their well-established personalities, although some surprises are presented by the author.

12. Newman, Bernard. *Shoot!* London: Gollancz, 1949. 241 pp.

It is hard to think that the exhausted nations of Europe would have gone to war again in 1949, but Newman's early novel offers a scenario that anticipates later views of a future European land war. Characters are on the scene, but their role is only to assist in the unfolding of the plot. The Soviets, with superior numbers, are successful at first. They take most of continental Europe and move into the Middle East to capture important oil fields. The Western Powers are able to reverse the situation with superior technology, and they win in the end. Some particular ideas worth noting are the infiltration of antiwar groups by communists, the superiority of missiles to bombs carried by airplanes, and the miniaturization of atomic weapons. Nuclear bombs are dropped by both sides, and on one occasion, the Soviet Union overcomes the Western technological edge to deliver an explosive device by stealth. There is little to say for the literary style here; long sentences formed into short paragraphs march relentlessly across the pages without much variation. The book's strength lies in its broad-ranging and often accurate predictions about future weapons and strategy.

13. Orwell, George. *1984*. London: Secker & Warburg, 1949. 312 pp. LC 49-25253. Other Editions: New York: Harcourt, Brace, 1949, 314 pp. LC 49-9278, plus numerous other editions.

War has its role in Orwell's famous novel. While the hero, Winston, struggles to achieve and maintain some individual identity in the totalitarian society dominated by Big Brother, his country, Oceana, is at war first with Eurasia, then with Eastasia. The change of national enemies requires a rethinking and rewriting of history. Because the war is a main focus of national attention and a centerpiece of Hate Week activities in Oceana, the full array of war propaganda is brought into play. This propaganda campaign serves well as an important element in this authoritarian version of the future. *1984* certainly reflects Orwell's perceptions of the need of totalitarian societies for war.

1950–1959

1950

14. Fischer, Leonard. *Let out the Beast*. Toronto, Canada: Export Publishing, 1950. 159 pp.

The descent of man into savagery after a nuclear war occurs almost immediately and with near-enthusiasm in this unusual Canadian novel. The world war of 1965 pits Americanada against Europasia in an exchange of atomic bombs. In North America, little more than rubble is left as two survivors, Greg and Hillary, adjust to their new circumstances by killing virtually everyone with whom they come into contact. In some cases, they murder before they themselves are slaughtered, but at other times, they ambush other scavengers in order to loot their bodies. Greg and Hillary make their abode in a cellar and live little better than rats. After Hillary dies in childbirth, Greg lives on for another 15 years. He accumulates a large family and establishes a reputation as a fierce fighter and a good provider. The latter task grows easier as the land begins to heal itself, and crops and small game reappear in abundance. Finally, Greg is killed as he attempts to steal a woman from a more civilized and disciplined group. *Let out the Beast* is notable for especially lurid cover art, but the review copy is so badly printed that it is illegible in parts.

15. Guerard, Albert J. *Night Journey*. New York: Knopf, 1950. 357 pp.

Several times in this novel, one of the narrators reminds himself to stop digressing and get on with the story. Unfortunately, neither he nor the author is able to do that, so what may be an interesting discussion of values, trust, and loyalty in war is lost among thousands of words that contribute nothing. Paul Haldane is an aide to a political officer in an undeclared but active conventional war somewhere in Europe. The officer attempts to establish a socialist civilian government in a newly occupied city. Haldane abandons the officer during a bombardment and is later detained by military authorities. During interrogation, Haldane and his questioner relate everything each has done, seen, or thought in his lifetime—or nearly so. It emerges that the motives of every individual and group may be questioned, and many are. At the end, most of the principal characters are dead.

16. Merril, Judith. *Shadow on the Hearth*. Garden City, NY: Doubleday, 1950. 277 pp. LC 50-8437. Other Edition: London: Sidgwick & Jackson, 1953, 287 pp.

It does not take a radical feminist of the 1980s to object to the female characters in this novel. When major American cities are hit with an unexpected atomic attack, Gladys, the young housewife who is the central character, reacts by becoming hysterical, wondering repeatedly where her husband might be while fearing the worst in detail, and attempting, with consistent failure, to control an unbelievably ill-mannered child. The bombs have torn Gladys's world apart, and she joins other women in falling to pieces emotionally. Yet, in the context of the novel, she is intended to be a heroine. In the days following the attack, Gladys pulls herself and her family together enough to cope with a new world run by civil defense authorities. A daughter's radiation sickness is the basis for a good deal of specific material about appropriate medical treatment, and a male doctor enters the story as a supporting character. There is little relief for the reader from the tension and panic that are sustained throughout. Characteristically, common sense and purposeful activity usually emerge only from the occasional male characters. Throughout, brief chapters allude to the effort of the husband to make it home. Torn, bloody, and wounded, he arrives just as the radio announces America's victory at the end of the war.

1951

17. Dubois, Theodora. *Solution T-25*. Garden City, NY: Doubleday, 1951. 218 pp. LC 51-1623. Other Edition: New York: Modern Literary Editions, 197?.

It may comfort some to learn that Theodora Dubois expects the upper classes to survive the next war. The characters in *Solution T-25* react to nuclear war and Soviet occupation in the manner of students at a prep school that has just employed a particularly harsh headmaster. Working in New York and Florida, the American resistance develops a drug that causes amiability and then introduces it into the food of senior occupation officers. The effect is to turn them from two-dimensional beasts into two-dimensional fools. The final stage of the drugging is timed to coincide with the counterattack of American forces from the unoccupied western portion of the U.S. In this novel, as in many others, Denver is chosen as the alternative U.S. capital after Washington is attacked and occupied. Subplots have to do with a drastic love affair and a group of orphan children whose purpose may be to add to the troubles of the principal characters.

18. Gibbs, Lewis. *Late Final*. London: J.M. Dent, 1951. 216 pp.
For about a year, probably sometime in the 1950s, the narrator Carey lives in a part of England devastated and depopulated by a war that is barely mentioned. Carey arrives in rural Hampshire by an unlikely means, having been a prisoner in Russia for 10 years. He is taken in by a surviving landowner and accepted as part of a household that numbers some 10 people. The story is as much about people as it is about a society in the aftermath of war. Carey indulges in lengthy philosophical speculation and plays at romance with a teenage girl. Reality enters the situation in the form of sheep thieves and other raiders who force the household into a military defense. Carey survives a destructive gunfight and is rescued by an American, whom he appears to resent for no clear reason. At the end, he is in a Roman Catholic monastery in New England. Throughout, *Late Final* is very slowly paced. Much of it could be a straightforward story about rural England without the special circumstances of future war.

19. Tucker, Wilson. *The City in the Sea*. New York: Rinehart, 1951. 250 pp. LC 51-13119/L. Other Edition: New York: Galaxy Publishing, 1951, 159 pp.
The atomic destruction of America was some thousand years in the past. What seems to be old California is ruled by a female military order armed with bows and swords and mounted on horses. When a man wanders into the area from the unknown lands beyond the mountains, a troop of infantry is sent to explore. As 100 women follow their male guide into what seems to be the interior of the U.S., they find remnants of twentieth-century structures, and they encounter several groups of mutants, some of which exhibit startling physical characteristics, but they fit smoothly into the context of the story. Gradually, the male guide assumes control of the explorers and leads

them to a city populated by an advanced and long-lived race. The people of the city have expanded their minds to remember large blocks of twentieth-century scientific knowledge. They can also communicate telepathically and create illusions in the minds of others. What they need is women, and it is revealed that the apparent expedition of the women warriors has been nothing more than a herding operation by the man. All of the women volunteer to remain in the advanced civilization.

1952

20. Berry, Bryan. *Born in Captivity*. London: Hamilton, 1952. 192 pp.
The "captivity" of the title has to do with two totalitarian states that share control of the world between a future nuclear war in the 1960s and another in 2018. What was England is part of the Western Federation where the first war reduced population to a manageable level. The postwar government controls population through selective reproduction laws. Thought police ensure that citizens' activities are docile and that only approved forms of expression flourish. Humans are served by technology that appears both familiar and likely to a reader in the 1980s. This generally accurate vision of the scientific future is one of the book's best aspects. The main characters are a government agent and his wife who defect to an active resistance organization. A sanctuary of this group is a vast 1960s bomb shelter on the Isle of Man; it is here that they survive the world atomic war of the early twenty-first century. Weapons of the new war include manned bombers and conventional weapons but not intercontinental missiles. The war exhausts the two world governments, and the resistance movement, a truly international organization, emerges to inherit the ruins.

21. Caldwell, Taylor. *The Devil's Advocate*. New York: Crown, 1952. 375 pp. LC 52-5681.
In 1970, America is in the grip of a totalitarian regime. The cities are in decay, and the masses of citizens are virtual slaves in factories that produce supplies for a succession of world wars. Canada and Mexico have been absorbed into the United States, and there is an ongoing war with South America. With ideas formed by the old U.S. Constitution, a group of patriots called Minute Men manage to introduce dissatisfaction among favored elements of the ruling elite and incite a

revolution that restores the republic. The hero, Andrew Durant, and most others in the book, speak and think in cliche-ridden paragraphs of great length about life, citizenship, responsibility, and the idea of freedom. Much of the action is trivial, and there is no convincing sense of how the characters actually work out the great events for which they seem to be responsible.

22. Norton, Andre. *Star Man's Son.* New York: Harcourt, Brace, 1952. 248 pp. LC 52-6906/AC/L/r80. Other Editions: New York: Fawcett, 1952, 224 pp, ISBN 0449236145; London: Staples, 1953, 253 pp; London: Gollancz, 1968, 248 pp, LC 68-134821; Boston: Gregg, 1980, 253 pp, LC 79-26128/AC. Other Title: *Daybreak, 2250 A.D.* New York: Ace Books, 1952, 191 pp; New York: Ace Books, 1954, 182 pp. (Issued as a double novel with Kutter, H. *Beyond Earth's Gates.*)

Three hundred years after a nuclear holocaust, Fors is a member of a mountain tribe. Against the customs of his people, Fors embarks on a journey of exploration with Lura, his mutant hunting cat. Fors visits the ruined cities of the Old Ones and marvels at the remnants of their civilization. He also encounters the Beast Things, horrible mutants who live in the ruins and appear to be planning a migration to the plains and mountains. Fors makes an alliance with tribes of the plains against the Beast Things and is finally welcomed back to his mountain tribe. This readable novel features plausible and fully constructed societies and some entertaining scenes of action.

23. Reynolds, Philip. *When and If.* New York: William Sloan, 1952. 246 pp. LC 52-12145. British Title: *It Happened Like This.* London: Eyre and Spottiswoode, 1952, 191 pp.

This early French novel describes a Soviet invasion of Western Europe with conventional weapons along the lines of the German attack of 1940. The narrator is a Frenchman employed by the Anglo-American forces as a resistance organizer. After a year of war, the Soviets attack Britain and the U.S. with atomic weapons, and the two allies retaliate with nuclear attacks. There is a considerable exchange, and both sides agree to avoid using nuclear weapons in the future. The allies ultimately liberate Europe with a World War II type invasion. There is virtually no dialog in the novel, and no characters are developed except the narrator. While the translation is good, 61 very short chapters hurt continuity.

24. Tucker, Wilson. *The Long Loud Silence*. New York: Rinehart, 1952. 217 pp. LC 52-8742. Other Edition: New York: Dell, 1953, 193 pp.

Principal character Russell Gary is remarkably able to adapt to chaotic conditions when the eastern United States is attacked with atomic and biological weapons. Gary, a combat-experienced Army corporal, is cut off from his command. He cannot cross the Mississippi River because the surviving American government has established it as a barrier against refugees from the East who are infected with plague. The unnamed enemy does not invade, and conditions in the eastern states deteriorate over the years as the weak die out and the strong sharpen their survival skills. On a brief fling in the West, Gary discovers that although he is immune himself, he can infect with plague most other people he touches. In despair, he returns to the bombed-out East searching for a few friends he made since the attack. Gary's friends are dead or gone, but he lives on several years until he meets an old girlfriend. Together, these two seem able to handle whatever the future holds. The author deals with several heavy subjects, including rape, cannibalism, murder, and personal loyalty and plays them out with skill against the background of a countryside devastated by bombs and disease.

25. Wolfe, Bernard. *Limbo*. New York: Random House, 1952. 432 pp. LC 52-5165.

This is a remarkable book for 1952, offering scientific and social ideas that seem timely over 30 years later. The central character is Martine, a doctor who deserted American forces in 1972, during the Third World War, and who has lived for 18 years on an uncharted island. When he returns to North America in 1990, he finds that much of the United States was destroyed by nuclear and computer weapons. The remaining population lives in a new nation, the Inland Strip, in the center of the continent. The corresponding nation of survivors in Eurasia is the East Union. Citizens of both nations submit to a voluntary amputation so that arms and legs can be replaced with powerful artificial limbs. Martine also discovers that he has become a cult figure in the Inland Strip, where some of his former acquaintances have achieved political and social power. Soon, the East Union attacks the Inland Strip using, among other things, suitcase atomic bombs planted by traitors. As the war rages, Martine attempts to return to his island refuge. The author's breadth of knowledge is obvious, but the book fails as a novel because it is filled with moral and philosophical speculation, subplots, word play, and other bits of literary cleverness. All of this, however, is a rich speculative undertaking by what is clearly an original and powerful intellect.

1953

26. Kornbluth, C.M. *The Syndic*. Garden City, NY: Doubleday, 1953. 223 pp. LC 53-9984. Other Edition: New York: Bantam, 1955, 142 pp.

It is some 100 years in the future, and the United States is divided between two criminal gangs. The Mob controls the West, and the Syndic runs the East. Remnants of the North American Government exist as slaveholding pirates based in Ireland and Iceland. Government military forces make occasional raids on American territory and plan angrily for reconquest. Kornbluth assembles this wildly improbable scene with believability and internal consistency. Through the conversations of his characters, he makes a plausible case for the advantages of large criminal gangs over elected governments. Adventure is provided by Charles Orsino, scion of a ruling Syndic family, who is sent to spy on the Government. After a foray among the wild tribes of Ireland, he uncovers a conspiracy among the Government and the Mob to conquer the Syndic. Charles acquires a lover along the way and returns from his mission after many perils. In addition to a compelling story in an inventive setting, the book contains interesting and often accurate speculation about future technology.

27. Padgett, Lewis. *Mutant*. New York: Gnome Press, 1953. 210 pp. LC 53-12601.

"Baldies" are mutant telepaths born among human survivors after an atomic war called the Blowup. For some generations, the Baldies live carefully, avoiding the wrath of humans who mistrust them. In what was the United States, a civilization is rebuilt that allows very little formal government, supports no organized military, and achieves a high level of technical development. Populations are low, and some persons join tribes of wanderers, called Hedgehounds, who live in the huge forests that have reclaimed much of the continent. One group of telepaths, called Paranoids, plots to dominate normal humans while another group, the Mutes, seeks to stop them. In the context of this struggle, various individuals, both Baldies and human, work out their fates. Thoughts and communication by telepaths are handled adroitly, but values and hopes are conveyed with too much repetitive detail. At the climax, everyone's intentions—good and bad—appear to submit to the violence of a human mob. It is awkward that the whole structure of the postnuclear war world is not conveyed in a more definite manner because this book provides a unique and important setting for a complicated story.

1954

28. Bennet, Margot. *The Long Way Back*. London: Bodley Head, 1954. 206 pp. Other Editions: New York: Coward-McCann, 1955, 248 pp, LC 55-6515; London: Science Fiction Book Club, 1957, 206 pp.

A worldwide cataclysm 1,500 years before the story opens seems to have been a nuclear war. In Africa, an advanced civilization sends out an expedition to what had been Britain. After landing, some members of the expedition are killed by savage dogs. Others survive to view mutant animals until they encounter a people as primitive as those who greeted Caesar when he came to England centuries before. Much of the work is given over to conversations among the African explorers and with advanced persons among the natives. Time is spent fruitlessly searching for the ruins of cities that might contain remnants of the former English civilization. In the end, the explorers return to Africa, having failed to convince one of the Englishmen to join them. Some impression is conveyed that the visitors from a superior civilization have set the English on the long road toward recovery of their past greatness, but that is left vague. This book begins with an interesting idea, then goes nowhere.

29. Crowcroft, Peter. *The Fallen Sky*. London: Peter Nevill, 1954. 222 pp.

Greenery, encroaching on the ruins of London, plays a large part in the setting of this postholocaust pastoral. Only isolated individuals are left alive a few years after a nuclear war. The story deals with interaction among only two characters of any significance; there are no major encounters with other persons. Bob, a former sociologist, hunts dogs for food and in turn is hunted by them. Eve, a young woman, cares for a group of blind children. These two team up and build something of an optimistic life. The ruins of England are not an especially hostile environment for this group of survivors. The style is romantic and symbolic in a more heavy-handed sense than is usual in English writing. A final disappointment is that the war that precipitated this particularly reduced state of humanity is not described with any specificity.

30. Shafer, Robert. *The Conquered Place*. New York: G.P. Putnam's Sons, 1954. 313 pp. LC 54-7865.

For its time, this is a remarkably sophisticated and complete work of fiction. The Enemy, who are Russians in everything but name, have conquered all the world except the western United States and South America. Few details of the military background are present, but the U.S. has already used atomic bombs during its retreat from Europe. Now, a U.S. Army officer must penetrate a city in Ohio which has been occupied for six years to arrange the rescue of an important scientist. Although he has mediocre cooperation from the underground, this support dissolves when he reveals that an atomic bomb will cover the scientist's airborne escape. Shafer does a superb job of drawing his characters, building action incrementally toward a climax, and setting a credible and detailed scene in an American city under enemy occupation. When the bombing raid coincides with a resistance uprising, the threads of the story are drawn together ably, the characters act true to their personalities, and fate has an appropriate role. *The Conquered Place* is one of the best books read for this bibliography.

31. Wylie, Philip. *Tomorrow*. New York: Rinehart, 1954. 372 pp. LC 53-10924.

Sometime in the 1950s, the citizens of the American towns of River City and Green Prairie lead typical, almost idyllic middle-class lives. They also prepare for war according to government civil defense guidelines. War comes in the form of atomic bombs, missiles, and bacteria weapons. Military and civilian defense officials make heroic efforts, but defeat seems likely. Also, mobs are ravaging the countryside, and order is gradually breaking down. In a last effort, the original nuclear submarine, Nautilus, is converted to a huge hydrogen bomb and detonated in the Gulf of Finland. The explosion destroys most life in northern and central Soviet Union by radiation sickness. In two weeks, the remnant of the Soviet government surrenders. As Americans begin to pick up the pieces of their country, aid arrives from Europe and Latin America. Wylie's anticommunist rhetoric is rather heavy-handed, but the story is interesting in its exhaustive detail about how a typical family and community might deal with nuclear war.

1955

32. Brackett, Leigh. *The Long Tomorrow*. Garden City, NY: Doubleday, 1955. 222 pp. LC 55-9983.

The historic westward migration through the Ohio valley is re-created in this story set in the early twenty-first century after a late twentieth-century war. American society is kept rural and agricultural by a constitutional amendment banning settlements of over 1,000 people. Religious sects that stress the simple life dominate the country, but growing forces of industry, commerce, and science compete for popular attention. Len, a farm boy, grows to maturity in his search for Bartorstown, a scientific community in the Rocky Mountains. When he reaches that fabled spot, Len discovers that scientific progress through atomic power offers no more guarantees in the twenty-first century than it did in the previous one. One is left with the feeling that hope for the future is ambiguous. Brackett is an able writer with a fine ability to evoke the physical environment.

33. Kornbluth, C.M. *Not This August*. Garden City, NY: Doubleday, 1955. 190 pp. LC 55-8406/L. Other Editions: New York: Bantam, 1956, 165 pp; New York: Tom Doherty Associates, distributed by Pinnacle Books, 1981, 255 pp, ISBN 0523485182. British Title: *Christmas Eve*. London: Michael Joseph, 1956, 206 pp. Other Edition: London: Science Fiction Book Club, 1958, 206 pp.

Occupation by Soviet and Chinese troops follows an American military defeat in the near future. Whole cities have been destroyed, but the central problem for Americans is not the lingering effects of radiation but survival under a regime that aims to work and starve the population to death. Specific brutalities of Soviet soldiers in rural New York are described with brisk, convincing prose that characterizes the entire work. The hero, Billy Justin, is a small dairy farmer who finds himself caught up in a dangerous resistance plot. An American earth satellite, almost completed in secret before defeat, is armed with awesome nuclear weapons and launched at great peril by the conspirators. It represents a new level of military technology, and the Americans successfully use it to blackmail the Soviets and Chinese into relinquishing the fruits of their recent victory. The 1981 edition, revised by Frederick Pohl, eliminates dated technical material and provides interesting background about the author.

34. Mead, Harold. *The Bright Phoenix*. London: Michael Joseph, 1955. 184 pp. Other Edition: New York: Ballantine, 1956, 184 pp, LC 56-9577.

The war is a central event of history, over 120 years past when the story begins. The State is the only known human community. In it, authoritarian control ensures that no violence or disorder will emerge. Awkward citizens are processed into zombie-like Reconditioneds. To the east of the State lies the Island, much as in the relationship of England to continental Europe. When a party of State citizens and Reconditioneds begins to colonize the Island, they meet a primitive people who live in villages and use bows and arrows. These people include mutants, and they are short of females. A crude form of Christianity persists among them. The clash of cultures leads to war, and the Islanders win at least the first few battles. Affairs are by no means settled at the end of the story.

35. Sohl, Jerry. *Point Ultimate*. New York: Rinehart, 1955. 185 pp. Other Edition: New York: Bantam, 1959, 151 pp.

By 1999, the enemy has occupied the United States and the rest of the world for 30 years. They have attacked major American cities with atomic weapons and blocked retaliatory bombers and missiles with a new force-field technology. To enforce their brutal control of the U.S. population, the enemy (who are clearly the Russians) infect everyone with plague, which requires monthly shots to avoid death. A young man who knows he is immune to the plague sets off from his home in rural Ohio to find a resistance movement whose existence is only rumored. After many adventures, he manages to join the resistance and learns that it is much more powerful and able than he ever imagined. The plot and action are competent, and some of the scientific devices of the future are interesting. Characterization is rather weak, and at the end of the book, the reader knows and cares little more about the hero and his friends than at the beginning.

1956

36. Caiden, Martin. *The Long Night*. New York: Dodd, Mead, 1956. 242 pp. LC 56-6287.

Civil defense is an occasionally controversial issue in the United States, especially because there are only the most rudimentary plans for civilians in time of war. The matter was more in the public eye in the 1950s, and this novel depicts a relatively well-organized system of civil defense in Harrington, a manufacturing city in northeastern United States. When the city is attacked by Soviet airplanes with atomic weapons, the initial destruction and later radiation are devastating. Many citizens who are not killed or injured panic, but a well-prepared civil defense organization takes over and manages to control the situation and limit damage. Central characters are members of the Thompson family who attempt to reunite in the chaos following the attack. The novel covers only a 24-hour period after the bombing, and most of it is given over to emotional sermonizing about the essential goodness of Americans and the value of well-organized civil defense. Descriptions of the effects of bombing are graphic, but this book is not a conceptually sophisticated work.

37. Frank, Pat. *Forbidden Area*. 1st ed. Philadelphia: Lippincott, 1956. 252 pp. LC 56-6417. Other Editions: Philadelphia, PA: Lippincott, 1956, 221 pp; New York: Bantam, 1957, 213 pp. British Title: *Seven Days to Never*. London: Constable, 1957, 252 pp.

In this novel by the author of the better-known Alas, Babylon (1959, entry 52), a Soviet attack on the U.S. is averted in part by a limited naval war. U.S. task forces sink Soviet submarines approaching North America. The story has two interesting ideas. The first is that the Soviets are anxious to attack before a presumably unbeatable U.S. ICBM is employed (shades of the MX). The second is a plan for Soviety agents in the Strategic Air Command to ground long-range bombers by a form of sabotage which simulates equipment failure. The characters are civilians and servicemen, mostly from the Air Force, in a government bureau charged with estimating Soviety intentions. Despite resistance from unbelieving bureaucrats higher up, they manage to save the day. Cities are evacuated, and Soviety submarines are destroyed at sea. The Soviets ultimately back down, and nuclear war is avoided.

38. Herbert, Frank. *The Dragon in the Sea*. New York: Avon, 1956. 189 pp. Other Titles: *21st Century Sub,* New York: Avon, 1956; Garden City, New York: Doubleday, 1956, 192 pp, LC 56-5586; London: Gollancz, 1960, 206 pp; Harmondsworth, England: Penguin, 1963, 218 pp; *Under Pressure,* New York: Ballantine, 1974, 220 pp.

The 1974 title of this excellent novel is the most descriptive, for both water pressure and psychological pressure are predominant in stories about submarines. Since it was written nearly 30 years ago, this is a good naval adventure that shows clearly its author's ability to craft engaging, heroic characters. But Herbert conveys more notable ideas here as well. He predicts the use of oil as a major factor in economic and military war. The novel takes place early in the twenty-first century, and America leads the Western powers in a war against the Eastern bloc that has already lasted for 16 years. The four-man crew of a submarine tug tows a giant underwater barge to steal oil from Soviet offshore wells. They search among themselves for a traitor as they battle the sea and enemy vessels. Technical emergencies may occur too frequently and in excessive detail, but Herbert makes remarkably accurate guesses about the shape of future tools and weapons.

39. Jones, Raymond. *The Secret People*. New York: Avalon, 1956. 224 pp. LC 56-13307.

Despite its grandiose presentation, this account of a struggle between a mutant father and his son is unique and touching. It is set in the future, perhaps 100 years after a nuclear war that destroyed major cities and left substantial latent radiation. Another legacy of the war are mutants who conceal themselves from humans. A genetic engineer based in Kansas City is actually a secret telepathic mutant. Over a period of 35 years, he substitutes his own sperm for that of human donors in a worldwide artificial insemination scheme. When human genetic police close in, the engineer escapes to a secret colony of his mutant children and learns that his eldest son, the colony leader, plans to take the mutants to another planet. The father feels that they should remain on earth to help the humans rebuild society. After a symbolic struggle with his son for leadership, the father is given the opportunity to evaluate whether the earth and its remaining human population deserve help. Several subplots with a variety of premises enrich this fascinating novel.

40. Monsarrat, Nicholas. *The Tribe that Lost Its Head*. New York: William Sloan, 1956. 598 pp. LC 56-9018.

This novel is a fine piece of writing that describes an armed insurrection of Africans against British colonial rule. Pharamaul is an imaginary island off the southwest coast of Africa, but it might well be Kenya in the early days—before the Mau Mau. A native population has good but not compelling reasons to be dissatisfied with a paternalistic British administration. Also included in the plot are a young, well-educated tribal chief, a few communist agitators, and some ugly racial incidents. The principal villain is a yellow journalist who exacerbates tensions in order to make news stories. Later, a few other itinerant leftist troublemakers arrive on the island and make a bad situation worse. Members of the government are generally rendered favorably; they know what is best for the natives and are doing fine jobs under the circumstances. When unrest turns into a particularly brutal insurrection, local forces, led by a naval officer, mount a superb expedition to relieve a captured town. Government forces are then able to control the situation until regular infantry units arrive from England. When this long book is read in the context of events since 1956, Monsarrat emerges as a talented writer with a sound view of political trends in Africa.

41. Richards, Guy. *Two Rubles to Times Square.* New York: Duell, Sloan, & Pearce, 1956. 206 pp. British Title: *Brother Bear,* London: Michael Joseph, 1957.

Invasion by stealth forms the basis for this interesting novel that is set almost entirely in New York City. A renegade Soviet general, Ketov, manages to bring a division of the Red Army ashore from disguised transport ships and occupy the southern portion of the city without significant resistance. He claims to want peace and understanding between the U.S. and his country. After some dithering about hostages and financial institutions under Ketov's control, American military forces assault and defeat the invaders. Thousands of the latter loot banks and flee throughout the nearby countryside in civilian clothes. Some are captured, but most surrender at Ketov's instructions after he is taken into American custody. Ketov then attempts to persuade the U.S. government to employ his unit as a sort of American foreign legion, but the decision is made to deport him and his followers back to Russia. The Navy intends to transport them via the Mediterranean, where they will have several opportunities to escape from custody and remain in the West. A notable feature of this implausible book is that Soviet officers are portrayed as sensitive, caring individuals rather than as brutes.

1957

42. Barlow, James. *One Half of the World.* New York: Harper & Row, 1957. 277 pp. LC 56-11097. Other Edition: London: Cassell, 1957, 214 pp.

The Occupiers of England are Russians in all but name. After a successful invasion of continental Europe, they have defeated Great

Britain with weapons that might have been nuclear, biological, or both. Some three years after the invasion, the Occupiers have imposed a regime that is drab and authoritarian, but not egregiously cruel. Many people find that their new government is better in some ways than the former system of class distinction and economic inequality. One of these people is Baxter, an internal security officer, who works against a resistance movement that is supported by the United States. Baxter is converted to the rebels' cause through an unconvincing and almost perfunctory combination of romance and religion. The details of conspiracy and police routines are also implausible. Conversations about desperate matters are artificial and structured, and characters in life and death situations pay no attention at all to secrecy. When Baxter's treason is discovered by fellow officers, he sacrifices himself to save the woman he loves and her family. These few escape, but back in England the future belongs to the Occupiers.

43. Cole, Burt. *Subi, The Volcano*. New York: Macmillan, 1957. 220 pp. LC 57-9365.

The possibility that the United States might be victorious in an Asian land war is remote in view of recent events, but it provides the essentials of setting and plot for Cole's realistic and exciting novel. In the near future, a major U.S. base is in a ruined city in an unnamed Asian country. It is a fetid, rotting, starving place with a large, hostile refugee population. The social and cultural differences between the Americans and Asians are reminiscent of the Vietnam War. Tactically, too, it is a case of regular troops with conventional weapons trying to fight an elusive enemy on its own ground. Military innovations include subcaliber rifles, battlefield television, fabric armor, and the extensive use of tunnels. The morale of American troops weakens steadily as enemy strength grows. As well as a story of future war, this might be a historical novel about a continually deteriorating military situation far from home. Cole is a good stylist with the ability to represent military circumstances and personalities accurately.

44. Moore, Catherine. *Doomsday Morning*. Garden City, NY: Doubleday, 1957. 216 pp. LC 57-12471/L. Other Editions: New York: Avon, 1957, 221 pp; London: World Distributors, 1960, 192 pp; New York: Avon, 1968, 208 pp.

Set at the beginning of the twenty-first century, this book features the aftermath of the Five-Day War, which has been over for about 30 years. Little information is given about the war, for instance the enemies and victors are not named, but it has paved the way for a presidential dictatorship, which operates through Comus, a governmental communications, transportation, and police organization. Howard Rohan, an alcoholic former actor and director, is caught up in a rebellion against Comus, centered in California. Rohan is an interesting character who is beset by personal problems that sometimes loom larger in the story than the struggle between Comus and the rebels. Although it is sometimes stretched rather thin, the central idea of the importance of communications in operating a modern state is ahead of its time. Even though the characters sometimes get in the way of the story, *Doomsday Morning* offers some challenging concepts about future rebellion after a future war.

45. Shute, Nevil. *On the Beach*. New York: William Morrow, 1957. 320 pp. LC 57-9158. Other Editions: Melbourne, Australia: Heinemann, 1957, 312 pp.; New York: New American Library, 1958, 238 pp; Toronto, Canada: Bantam Books, 1968, 278 pp; London: Heron Books, 197?, 311 pp; New York: Scholastic Book Services, 1972, 234 pp; New York: Ballantine, 1974, 278 pp.

Due in part to the motion picture based on this novel, the Australian setting for the end of life on earth is one of the best-known visions of World War III. The destructive atomic war has occurred about a year before the story begins. An Arab-Israeli war leads to a NATO-Warsaw Pact conflict that in turn sparks a Soviet-Chinese confrontation. Poisonous radiation blankets the Northern Hemisphere and is inexorably drifting south toward the survivors in Australia. The central characters are sailors, especially the officers and crew of the U.S.S. Scorpion, a nuclear submarine that is sent north to survey the devastated areas. Throughout the book, characters know that the end is coming within six months, and they react variously with resignation, nobility, and cowardice. As they become ill with radiation poisoning, their individual modes of death take on more significance because they know that their deaths are part of the death of all humankind. Shute's construction of an end for the world is eminently plausible, and his excellent characterization contributes to a fine novel.

1958

46. Bryant, Peter. *Red Alert*. New York: Ace Books, 1958. 191 pp.
This is clearly a more primitive version of *Dr. Strangelove* (1964, entry 76), a novel that also bears Bryant's name. The essential story is the same: an American bomber, launched by a mad general, penetrates Russian defenses and drops a nuclear bomb. In this version, the results are less catastrophic than in *Dr. Strangelove,* and general worldwide destruction is averted. Even so, there is plenty of deadly action between U.S. and Russian forces and between different elements of the American military. The plot and characters here are uninspired, and there is none of the cynical humor of the later work. In terms of literary quality, *Red Alert* is similar to *Commander-1* (1965, entry 85), a future war novel written by Bryant under his real name of Peter George.

47. Coon, Horace. *43,000 Years Later*. New York: New American Library, 1958. 143 pp.
A story set among extraterrestrial beings tens of thousands of years in the future would normally be outside the scope of this bibliography. However, in this epistolary account, the characters are exploratory archeologists, scouting the planet Earth long after a war that has left nothing alive but insects. The observations and comments of these beings offer a satirical perspective on human nature, history, nationalities, and political institutions. The final war is discovered to have been a predictable East/West conflict that occurred in 1957 and led to the exchange of 240 hydrogen weapons. While the interplanetary archeologists come to have some understanding and affection for the long-doomed humans, they recognize the danger of the destructive impulse that dominated and finally destroyed that species.

48. Jones, Ewart C. *Head in the Sand*. London: Arthur Barker, 1958. 223 pp.
This book has a hero who is in a permanent, agonizing dither of self-doubt. He wonders incessantly and at great length about what is right, and he must, in fact, be forced into any action by other characters. Once John Clayton is drawn into an active resistance movement against the Soviets who occupy Britain, he argues regularly against plans and refuses to obey orders. In any actual conspiracy, such an ineffective blabbermouth would be shot out of hand. Indeed,

several other characters consider just that, but in the end, it matters little because the nationwide uprising fails, and the Soviets prevail. This revolt occurs in the late 1960s or early 1970s, and there is comprehensive and thorough background about the development of Soviet domination of Europe. Numerous scenes of infantry combat between British and Soviet forces are handled with competence and technical accuracy. The book is noteworthy because the heroic, democratic resistance fighters do not achieve a miracle; instead they lose to the big battalions.

49. Jones, Merwyn. *On the Last Day*. London: Jonathan Cape, 1958. 266 pp.
The sense of impending doom is so realistic here because it is felt by civilized and reflective characters and conveyed in an erudite style. The year is 1959, and the British government is in exile in Quebec. The Soviets and Chinese are winning a war that has seen the use of both conventional and atomic weapons. Continental Europe and the British Isles are occupied by the Soviets, fighting continues in Africa, and Soviet bombers occasionally reach the coast of Canada. With the U.S., the British have built an intercontinental rocket with a hydrogen warhead that is intended for use against Soviet launching stations near London. Although they, too, are anticommunist, members of a Quebec separatist group act against the British scientists and officials involved with the missile. The people who are busy with these life and death matters also pursue their private lives. They play music, make love, and try to plan for a future that may not occur. *On the Last Day* is among the few future war novels that are worth reading for literary merit alone.

50. Rigg, Robert B. *War—1974*. Harrisburg, PA: Military Service Publishing, 1958. 304 pp. LC 58-6846.
On New Year's Day 1974, Russo-Chinese Eurasian forces attack the U.S. with ICBMs carrying nuclear warheads. The Eurasian troops also invade Western Europe. The United States retaliates with a bewildering array of superweapons. Battles are fought on land, sea, and in the air. The superior technology and tactics of the American military force a Eurasian surrender within a year. The plot is simple, and all of the human characters are perfunctory; many appear only briefly. The real characters are the weapons of the future, and they are predicted with some accuracy by the author, a serving Army officer. The emphasis on weapons is extended with numerous footnotes and

"factual" sections throughout the novel that further discuss weapons and tactics. There are also drawings and photographs to illustrate the author's ideas about the future development and employment of weapons. Colonel Rigg is no doubt a practiced writer of military prose, and he has obviously given much thought to his subject. However, he and his publisher did not choose wisely when they selected this format of semifiction to convey his predictions. Full of interesting content, the book is a hybrid that is most difficult to read. More conventional decisions about format and rigorous editing could have done much to produce a better book from such well-researched material.

1959

51. Foster, Richard. *The Rest Must Die*. New York: Fawcett, 1959. 176 pp.

In the first 40 days after a nuclear attack on New York City, a few thousand individuals survive in the subway system and in the basements of large buildings. These New Yorkers are remarkably calm, well ordered, and docile. A leadership group emerges that includes former police officers, air raid wardens, and a few strong personalities. There is a criminal element and some fights occur over food and women, but most characters accept the situation with equanimity. When some survivors emerge in New Jersey, they make contact with a government plane. They learn that the war is over and that only major cities in the U.S. and the Soviet Union have been destroyed. At a refugee camp in Virginia, some hardy characters plan to move west and begin life anew.

52. Frank, Pat. *Alas, Babylon*. Philadelphia, PA: Lippincott, 1959. 254 pp. LC 59-5405. Other Editions: New York: Bantam, 1960, 1964, 1970, 1976, 1979.

Pat Frank draws heavily on the institutions, characters, and activities of the Old West in this story set in Florida after a future nuclear war. Fort Repose is well named, for the bombs and fallout miss it, few sick people are in evidence, and the main result of the war is one of physical isolation. Randy Bragg, a lawyer and reserve officer, assumes local leadership in the days after the bombs fall. He organizes civic and economic institutions, forms a vigilante troop, and dispenses rough frontier justice to evildoers. Bragg and his followers adjust easily to life without modern conveniences and generally make do with the hardy spirit of pioneers. Although they do not verbalize the feeling at any length, one has the impression that these survivors are almost happier after the war than they were before. When an aircraft finally reaches them from what remains of the federal government, they decline evacuation to a more civilized area and express only mild interest in knowing who won the war.

53. Kirst, Hans Helmut. *The Seventh Day*. Translation of *Keiner Kommt Davon*. Garden City, NY: Doubleday, 1959. 424 pp. LC 52-8267/L. Other Editions: New York: Ace Books, 1959, 383 pp; New York: Pyramid, 1968, 382 pp. British Title: *No One Will Escape*. London: Weidenfel and Nicholson, 1959, 412 pp.

In view of the events in Poland in 1981–82, it is interesting that this account of the prelude and beginning of World War III begins with an outbreak of fighting between Polish and Soviet troops. Unrest spreads quickly to Germany, where soldiers on both sides of the border begin fighting against their standing orders. Despite efforts of NATO and some Soviet authorities, the situation escalates in a few days to a full nuclear war with intercontinental attacks on the U.S. and the Soviet Union. The Soviet advantages of men and material in Central Europe provide them with overwhelming early victories, and the NATO forces respond with tactical nuclear weapons. Through this dismaying course of events, Kirst guides the fate of 10 characters, all caught in events beyond their power. A minor flaw, common to translations, is that the dialog of American characters sounds completely unrealistic. Otherwise, this is a work of technical excellence and chilling content.

54. Roshwald, Mordecai. *Level 7*. New York: McGraw-Hill, 1959. 186 pp. LC 60-8115/L. Other Editions: New York: McGraw-Hill [Book club edition], 183 pp; New York: New American Library, 143 pp.

In a body of literature that is generally pessimistic, this book stands out as one of the first of a truly pessimistic nature. Because of its popularity, it has been reviewed and discussed frequently and favorably. Even so, it is tedious. Its essential political messages are that war is bad and governments are not humane; however, frequent repetition causes these messages to become trite. The story deals with a military officer in an unnamed country who is virtually imprisoned in the seventh and lowest level of a vast shelter complex. His job is to push buttons that launch atomic rockets against the enemy in case of war. Well over half the book describes how the officer and his colleagues make their various social and psychological adjustments to life underground. This happens over a period of several months. The war, when it comes, may have been triggered by a mistake, and the devastating response seems to be automatic. In the four months that follow, radiation gradually drifts down through the upper levels of the complex, and the personnel on Level 7 receive radio messages from their dying comrades above. Ironically, death comes to those on the lowest level as a result of an accident with their own nuclear reactor. While the message and values of this book are in agreement with the ideas of many people, its diary form contributes to its overall heavy handedness.

1960–1969

55. Casewit, Curtis W. *The Peacemakers*. New York: Avalon, 1960. 224 pp.

There is some internal confusion as to whether the story is set in 1970 or 1976, but in either case, many of the characters have adult memories of World War II. Virtually all have fought in World War III, which lasted several years and destroyed most of the world. To Rockland, an island refuge, come scientists of various nationalities. Upon arrival, they find that the former democratic government has been deposed by Herb Puckett, a former U.S. Army sergeant who is now a military dictator. Puckett forces the scientists to manufacture nerve gas for his forthcoming war with Sunland, a neighboring state. In secret, the scientists also develop an antiaggression substance. When the war comes, they administer it secretly to Rockland's forces and stop the war. All of this is conceptually simple, and the characters are utterly wooden. The single exception is Puckett, the villain. Although the man is evil, he has the only discernible personality in the book.

56. Coppel, Alfred. *Dark December*. Greenwich, CT: Fawcett, 1960. 208 pp.

Those who think that nuclear war might be survivable can find support in this grimly realistic novel of life in the U.S. at the close of a two-year war with the Soviet Union. Set in the 1970s, it is the story of Gavin, a former Air Force missile officer, who searches for his wife and children in the wasteland of radiation and social collapse that was Northern California. The novel is successful at several levels. First, the setting is convincing. The results of war are uneven on both people and nature rather than the universal chaos that is often conveyed in simpler works. Next, it is a good adventure story with plausible situations and characters who think and communicate as distinct, complete individuals. Finally, Gavin confronts his wartime role as a missile launch officer in the context of the destruction that enemy missiles have brought to his own homeland. Although the book is now over two decades old, its characters and outlook are by no means dated.

57. Hartley, L. P. *Facial Justice*. Garden City, NY: Doubleday, 1960. 263 pp.

For some decades after World War III, the people of Kent, England, some two million of them, live underground in shelter caverns. When it is discovered that the surface is inhabitable again, about half of them leave the caverns to form a new state under the benevolent Dictator. Through social pressure and regimentation of bodies and minds, the Dictator keeps his people occupied in harmless pursuits and trivial discussions. World War III has destroyed most existing structures and altered the weather to a permanent March climate, and in the barren wet cold environment very little grows. Ultimately, social discontent arises and the Dictator, who has been heard by all but seen by none, is overthrown. Conversations and introspection are lengthy and convoluted in this book, which is interesting but difficult to follow.

58. Miller, Walter M. *A Canticle for Leibowitz*. Philadelphia, PA: Lippincott, 1960. 320 pp. LC 60-5735. Other Editions: New York: Bantam, 1961, 278 pp; London: Corgi, 1963, 278 pp.

Certainly one of the best known novels of the future, *A Canticle for Leibowitz* is also one of the best written. It follows the fortunes of a monastic order in the American Southwest from a new dark age a few centuries after a worldwide holocaust through the redevelopment of science and technology in the thirty-eighth century. The monks and other characters struggle with basic elements of the human spirit and intellect: faith, common humanity, loyalty, and scientific inquiry. The book has a superb plot and includes passages that are quite beautiful and moving. However, a small but important portion of the text is in Latin, and readers without knowledge of that language may have to guess at its meaning. Even in this thoughtful and grand vision of the future, the outcome of human experience is finally failure. At the end, nuclear war has begun again, and the monks dispatch a spacecraft with human and material stock to carry on their faith beyond the doomed planet Earth. Miller does not say whether the colonists take with them the essentially violent nature of man, but they are wise to gain at least an extension of fate.

59. Smith, George. *Doomsday Wing*. n.p.: Bridbooks, 1960?. 124 pp. Other Edition: Derby, CT: Monarch Books, 1963, 124 pp.

The review copy of this book lacks preliminary pages, but internal cataloging information suggests that it was first published in 1960. The story seems to occur in the mid-1960s. It is little more than an Air Force adventure story set in the context of World War III. Chris Tolliver, a colonel, is assigned to the top secret Doomsday Wing near Denver. His job is to launch cobalt bombs at the Soviet Union should ultimate worldwide destruction ever be ordered. Shortly after Tolliver is assigned, a Berlin incident provides an insane Russian officer with the opportunity to launch ICBMs under his control, and the war is on. After an initial exchange of rockets and bombs, the Soviet premier makes contact with the American president who reveals the existence of the cobalt weapons. Colonel Tolliver flies to Russia as part of an international agreement to end the war. Although millions of people die, the story ends well because the hero finds happiness and hope for the future with an old love.

1961

60. Galouye, Daniel F. *Dark Universe*. New York: Bantam, 1961. 154 pp. Other Editions: London: Gollantz, 1963, 183 pp; Boston: Gregg, 1976, 154 pp, LC 76-10435.

For most of this book, the hero Jared deals with the concept of sight in his conversations and thoughts. Jared is one of a group of cave dwellers who live in complete darkness. They are several generations removed from the original inhabitants of a huge U.S. underground survival complex that was sealed during a thermonuclear war. The survivors have developed a complicated social structure and religion in which Light is a god and Radiation a devil. In their underground world, they live as bats, sensing the shape of their surroundings by sound and echo. Jared is an adventuresome young man who finally makes his way to the surface and encounters humans from another shelter who are trying to coax the cave dwellers to the surface by persuasion and other means. Jared finally discovers that he, too, can see, and he decides to stay on the surface and face the world with his eyes open.

61. Hough, S.B. *Beyond the Eleventh Hour*. London: Hodder & Stoughton, 1961. 190 pp.

In this short novel, Hough conveys ably and in detail the escalation of a Chinese invasion of Nepal in 1962 into a worldwide nuclear war. Among his characters are average citizens of various nations as well as world leaders, including an American president modeled after John Kennedy. In anticipation of current Western military thinking, the NATO countries are forced to use tactical atomic weapons to counter the weight of Soviet and Chinese numbers. This soon leads to the use of strategic weapons, and most cities of the world are destroyed. The Soviets begin a systematic attack on American territory with cobalt bombs, and the Americans respond with a single, awesome device that destroys all of the Soviet Union. Central authority in America collapses under the additional weight of a combined Japanese and Chinese invasion of the West Coast and subsequent occupation of the country west of the Continental Divide. When most nations are exhausted—populations killed and economies destroyed—it is India, which stayed out of the war, that emerges as a dominant power along with China.

62. Sillitoe, Alan. *The General*. New York: Knopf, 1961. 189 pp. LC 60-53009.

Set in the near future, this book presents a conventional war that has been raging for four years between two European nations. Soldiers of one nation, the Gorsheks, capture a symphony orchestra on its way to entertain enemy troops. The existence of the orchestra is reported to the Gorshek general who imprisons the troupe and radios higher authorities for orders on their fate. He is soon informed that the musicians, like all prisoners, are to be killed. The general, who has some sense of culture, stalls while he has the orchestra perform for him and his officers. In the face of subsequent demands from his superiors that he report the completed executions, the general becomes mentally disturbed. He kills a staff officer, arms the members of the orchestra, and sends them back to their own lines. Ultimately, he is convicted of murder by his own side. Sillitoe crafts several interesting characters who struggle with the roles and power imposed upon them by war.

63. Wilson, Angus. *The Old Men at the Zoo*. London: Secker and Warburg, 1961, 352 pp. Other Editions: New York: Viking, 1961, 352 pp; Harmondsworth, England: Penguin, 1964, 344 pp.

Wilson's literate and subtle novel is set in present-day England where the staff of a London zoo work against the background of approaching war with united European powers. The dispute is over Britain's refusal to join a general political and economic system. When the United States and the Soviet Union fail to calm the situation, Europe attacks Britain with conventional weapons. Germ warfare is rumored but its use is deliberately left vague. Little is conveyed of military matters, but the effect of the war on the civilian population is described graphically. Britain succumbs, and the postwar government collaborates with Europe. The former democratic system of manipulative politicians was by no means good, and many surviving characters think that the new regime is neither ill-intentioned nor brutal. Times are lean, and members of the former upper classes are unhappy, but there is reason to hope for the future. To enjoy this technically fine piece of writing, Wilson obliges the reader to endure an insufferable narrator whose values and motives are so exquisitely pure that he is impossible to like or believe.

1962

64. Barron, D.G. *The Zilov Bombs*. London: A Deutsch, 1962. LC 63-6185. Other Edition: New York: Norton, 1963, 173 pp, LC 62-19004.
Resistance to enemy occupation is a frequent theme in British future war novels. In Barron's book, it is 1973, and the Soviets have invaded all of Europe after nuclear protestors caused democratic governments to disarm. Guy Elliot, a minor agricultural official in the collaborationist bureaucracy in rural England, is caught up reluctantly in the resistance movement. With American support, they plan to destroy the People's Parliament with a stolen nuclear weapon, which will be the signal for patriotic uprisings all over Soviet-occupied Europe and probably an American invasion. Elliot is a former nuclear protestor with moral values that require tedious evaluation of every proposed action. This reluctance about working with the rebels may be sensible because its members evince a dangerously relaxed attitude about security. There is some effective tension as the Soviets close in on the British resistance, and Elliot is in the middle. When the Soviets break in, he has temporarily persuaded himself that the British cause is just, and he pushes the button to detonate the bomb. The Soviet invasion is a background event, and significant military action occurs only at the

end of the novel. The Zilov bombs themselves are interesting, however, because they have blast and fallout characteristics similar to modern neutron bombs.

65. MacTyre, Paul. *Doomsday 1999*. New York: Ace Books, 1962. 158 pp. British Title: *Midge*. London: Hodder & Stoughton, 1962. 195 [i.e. 159] pp.

After 10 years of conventional war, the Chinese have extended loose domination over most of the world. In Britain, they contend with quasi-military Guards and ragged bands of hunters. One of the latter, Angus, is thrown together with Liu, a female Chinese officer, in an adventure on the depopulated and wasted landscape of Scotland. They encounter Chinese garrison troops, concentration camps, and a refuge of scientists. The most fascinating aspect of the book is the midges—swarming insects like flies or mosquitoes that have been altered by a nuclear accident. Although the midges can and do kill humans, they have other, more unusual abilities. They can induce telepathic communication between individuals and they adopt Angus and Liu to use as their human agents for the development of a new peaceful world. This rebirth of what is good in people is only beginning as the book ends, but the situation clearly offers much hope. MacTyre forms these rather strange ideas into a readable and dramatic book with an outlook that belies its American title.

66. Owen, Dean. *End of the World*. New York: Ace Books, 1962. 127 pp.

In this novel, a nuclear attack on the United States brings about a breakdown of governmental control and subsequent widespread civil disorder but not the end of the world as advertised in the title. The story, apparently based on the motion picture of the same name, describes the efforts of a typical American family to keep themselves alive and secure after the country is thrown into disarray by an atom bomb attack. The father, Harry, takes his wife and two teenage children into the California wilderness to await the restoration of law and order. He fights various individuals and groups in order to acquire weapons and supplies and to protect the women. While his son is of some help, his wife and daughter adapt reluctantly and badly to the new circumstances of life. Their attempts to maintain prewar social habits and behavior puts the family group into serious danger several times, and they seem never to learn. Few persons in the story are at their best or most generous; most are terrified, greedy, and dangerous.

The decline into barbarism is almost immediate, and only the strong survive. Harry and his family are finally able to fight their way to an area under control of the U.S. Army.

67. Roshwald, Mordecai. *A Small Armageddon,* 1962. 211 pp. LC 62-40452/L. Other Edition: New York: New American Library, 1976, 165 pp.
The small armageddon of the title occurs sometime in the near future. A nuclear submarine and a nuclear missile battery destroy one another in a single exchange of weapons. Led by their respective commanding officers, personnel at both nuclear facilities mutiny, declare themselves independent states, and begin to blackmail the world. Roshwald handles this idea with a light, cynical touch that includes genuine humor. Despite his unlikely characters and plot, Roshwald's message about nuclear weapons falling into the wrong hands is quite serious. He ends the book with scenes of nuclear blackmail being acted out by neo-Nazis in Germany and by a small state in Africa.

68. Schoonover, Lawrence. *Central Passage.* New York: William Sloan, 1962. 246 pp. LC 62-9298. Other Edition: New York: Dell, 1964, 192 pp.
Two major themes in the plot and three points of view in narration are a bit much for such a brief book, but Schoonover is a good writer, and he brings it all together in a satisfactory manner. In 1964, a 20-minute nuclear war occurs between the U.S. and the Soviet Union. Each side fights hard, and the destruction and loss of life are substantial. Much of the Isthmus of Panama is obliterated. Its destruction causes changes in ocean currents that in turn bring on a new ice age. A hastily formed world government restores the isthmus with underwater atomic explosions, and weather resumes its normal pattern. The second aspect of the story has to do with superhumans—called, illogically, "Intruders," who are born during the war. As they grow to age 20, the Intruders demonstrate mental and physical capabilities roughly twice those of normal humans. They naturally plan to take over the world, and the government, just as naturally, seeks them out and kills them. At the end, there are a few Intruders left, and they are still plotting.

1963

69. Ariss, Bruce. *Full Circle.* New York: Avalon, 1963. 224 pp.
About 250 years after a twentieth-century nuclear war, only the descendants of the original American Indian tribes remain alive on the

North American continent. One tribe, encamped on a large lake near Mt. Rushmore, encounters a white man emerging from the lake in a diving suit. He is one of the few remaining members of the last generation of subterranean survivors. Their ancestors had been chosen before the war for qualities of intellect and physique and sent into an elaborate shelter under Mt. Rushmore National Monument. The subterranean people are dying out, and the White man and his sister, with oddly distorted values from the present day, have difficulty adjusting to the pastoral Indian life. Eventually, the White man commits a murder and stays away from the tribe for several years. When he returns, he reports that most of the rest of the world is depopulated and that several other Indian tribes in North America are planning to employ some of the twentieth-century technology still preserved in the shelter. The characters communicate awkwardly—in long, improbable sentences—about moral philosophy. This is, however, a worthwhile book that offers a unique perspective on the Indians within the frontier theme that appears so often in future war novels.

70. Goldstone, Robert. *The Shore Dimly Seen.* New York: Random House, 1963. 241 pp. LC 63-7645.

A large private yacht is at sea in the Atlantic with seven passengers and a skeleton crew when a war begins with an attack by Hungary on Yugoslavia. From a meeting with an American submarine at sea, the yachtsmen learn that the war may have escalated to a worldwide atomic exchange. Because their radio is out, the passengers and crew cannot be sure about the war or its effects, and they think and converse at length about their best course of action. There is a good deal of adventure at sea, including a storm and an abortive mutiny, before the yacht finally makes its way toward the Maryland shore. There is no sign of shipping, the Coast Guard, or other normal seagoing activity, and overhead there is only a single military airplane. The reader is left with the thought that the war has, in fact, occurred and that the sailors face even greater adventure ashore.

71. Good, Charles H. *The Wheel Comes a Turn.* New York: Vantage Press, 1963. 224 pp.

Unfortunately, the rich and unsettling aggregation of ideas about the future contained in this book are buried under impenetrable language, wooden characters, and a repetitive and complex plot. The basic story has to do with the rise of a feminist dictatorship in the Soviet Union, which attacks the United States near the end of the twentieth century. In addition to hydrogen bombs, the Soviets employ cobalt weapons that exceed their expectations and sterilize much of the plant and animal life on earth. The Americans forbear from using their intact underground weapons in retaliation because it would only make the worldwide situation worse. Instead, nations concentrate on rebuilding living populations with the few remaining fertile representatives of each species. A subplot deals with an elite group of scientists who migrate first to the moon and later to a distant planet to preserve much that is good in human culture. Also loose in the book are extraordinary ideas, quite forcefully expressed, about sex, family life, artificial insemination, religion, and more.

72. Household, Geoffrey. *Thing to Love*. Boston: Little, Brown, 1963. 344 pp. LC 63-13454.

Guayanas is a small nation on the Pacific coast of South America where revolutions are a customary and relatively bloodless method of governmental change. In 1959, however, a new element is on the scene in the form of the Fifth Division, a unit with modern arms and competent training, led by General Kucera, a Czech refugee. When a leftist revolution breaks out against a pro-American government, Kucera employs his division against the rebels with brutal and successful competence. He cannot end the war by winning battles, and the customary patterns of politics assert themselves to bring the rebels into political power. Kucera surrenders and is saved from execution by a gallant naval officer. Household's particular strength is characterization, and he draws a sympathetic portrait of a European officer attempting to live up to world standards of military loyalty and professionalism in the indefinite and less rigid environment of South America. Descriptions of military events include enough detail and coherence to be understandable without much trivia about weapons and equipment.

73. Wylie, Philip. *Triumph*. Garden City, NY: Doubleday, 1963. 277 pp. LC 63-7705. Other Edition: Greenwich, CT: Fawcett, 1964, 240 pp.

World War III begins sometime after 1961 when Hungary invades Czechoslovakia. Despite televised conferences between Eastern bloc and Western leaders, the conflict escalates to a nuclear exchange that is utterly destructive in the Northern Hemisphere. In Connecticut, a group of 14 people survives in the lavish shelter prepared by Vance

Farr, a wealthy businessman. Much of the story takes place in the shelter as the occupants become accustomed to each other and to the enclosed but highly technical environment. They also speculate about the causes and extent of the war, and they attempt to make radio contact with other survivors. Outside, American and Soviet second-strike forces, especially submarines, fight on, and the Americans are finally victorious. After two years, the shelter inhabitants are rescued by Australians who inform them that the remaining nations in the Southern Hemisphere are planning a world government. Despite being laden with much of Wylie's personal philosophy, this is a detailed and engaging novel.

1964

74. Aldiss, Brian W. *Greybeard*. New York: Harcourt, Brace, World, 1964. 245 pp. LC 64-18276.
   Characters and the relationships among them are well developed in this story set in England in the mid-twenty-first century. The Accident of 1981 sterilized most creatures, including people, and the wars that followed were fought for possession of the few remaining children. Later, revolutions began the process of dissolution of all central governments and political authority. Greybeard and his wife, Martha, who are in their 50s, are among the youngest people left in England. As they wander through the primitive, almost medieval, landscape, they meet everywhere the depression of old people who know that they are the last of a dying species. As the end of the book approaches, Greybeard and the others become increasingly aware of children who hide in the forest and disguise themselves as animals. These creatures are not entirely human, but they represent the only shred of remaining hope.

75. Dick, Philip K. *The Penultimate Truth*. New York: Leisure Books, 1964. 174 pp. Other Editions: New York: Belmont, 1964, 174 pp; London: Cape, 1967, 254 pp, LC 68-94841; Harmondsworth, England: Penguin, 1970, 220 pp, ISBN 140031057; St. Albans, England: Triad Panther, 1978, 207 pp, ISBN 0586047875; New York: Dell, 1980, 238 pp, ISBN 0440169267.
   In 2025 A.D., the Third World War has been over for 13 years. This fact is known only to a few of the wealthy, landed aristocracy who live above ground on palatial rural estates reclaimed from radioactive

ruins. Beneath the earth, however, in large shelter complexes, hundreds of thousands of people continue to build robots and other machines to fight a war they believe still continues. Most of the book is set among the aristocracy of the surface world, and the plot deals with struggles among them for access to life-prolonging artificial body parts. There are also elements of time travel and superhuman mental abilities. The various fantastic elements engage the reader's interest, but no themes are developed fully enough to be satisfying. Each page seems to present a new set of problems and opportunities unrelated to the "reality" already established. The characters spend much of their time thinking or expressing observations about the morality of their situation.

76. George, Peter. *Dr. Strangelove*. New York: Bantam, 1964. 145 pp. LC 63-15529. Other Edition: Boston: Gregg, 1979, 145 pp, LC 79-12237. This novelization of the 1964 motion picture by the same name is an exercise in black humor. A renegade Air Force commander sends a wing of nuclear bombers against the Soviet Union. When horrified civilian officials discover the action, they cooperate with the Russians so that all but one of the planes are shot down or recalled. Unfortunately, the plane that survives drops a bomb that in turn triggers a Russian doomsday machine—a nuclear weapon designed to wipe out all life on earth within a year. At the end of the story, American civilian and military leaders are cleverly plotting to secure themselves and selected females in long-term buried shelters. In an excellent introduction to the Gregg reprint edition, Richard Gid Powers argues persuasively that George, author of *Red Alert* (1958, entry 46) and *Commander-1* (1965, entry 85), lacked the skill to write *Dr. Strangelove*. Powers attributes much of the literary quality of this book to scriptwriter Terry Southern.

77. Heinlein, Robert A. *Farnham's Freehold*. New York: G.P. Putnam's Sons, 1964, 315 pp. LC 64-18007. Other Editions: New York: Berkeley, 1964, 1971, 320 pp; New York: New American Library, 1965, 256 pp; London: Denis Dobson, 1965, 315 pp.
Hugh Farnham is a self-made man who leads a group of family and friends into his well-prepared fallout shelter as a nuclear war begins in the near future. They live through the war and find that they have been transported hundreds of years into the future. The future world is governed by blacks who enslave and eat whites. Farnham's adven-

tures in the future are concluded when he manages to have himself, his mistress, and their children transported back to a time in the past just before the nuclear war. The parents and children are able to gather together enough necessities and retreat to a convenient mineshaft so that they can survive the same nuclear war once again. Their second time around involves no travel to the future. They emerge into the blasted and devastated planet to establish a trading post catering to the few other survivors in the primitive new frontier.

78. Miller, Warren. *The Siege of Harlem*. New York: McGraw-Hill, 1964. 166 pp. LC 64-22974.

The point of view here is that of an old man, telling his grandchildren about the liberation of Harlem many years ago. Some minor military action is recounted at length, but its result is only the capture of a single black infiltrator. A much larger invasion by the Colored Invasion Army is mentioned at several points, but the longest account covers only two pages. It is a conventional, small-unit infantry action that is won by the insurgents. In its context as a story told to children, the old man's tale is general rather than specific, so details about the political and social context of the Harlem insurrection are sparse. Miller's emphasis is clearly on the positive, and he effectively combines irony with gentleness. A welcome absence is any tone of stridency or bitterness. His restraint in handling matters about which he justifiably has strong feelings contributes to the effectiveness of the book.

79. Minot, Stephen. *Chill of Dusk*. Garden City, NY: Doubleday, 1964. 327 pp. LC 64-19236.

Fifty years after the end of World War III, approximately 50 survivors and their offspring live in the primitive community of Phoenix Colony in the forest of what was Maine. The colony leader, a man named Adams, preserves books and other records of prewar civilization and attempts to run a school. The old knowledge of literature, history, and philosophy is not, however, suited to the rough and immediate needs of farmers, wood-gatherers, and hunters. Amid philosophical introspection and conversation so complex and repetitive as to be boring, the citizens of the colony turn from Adams and the culture he represents to a primitive Roman Catholic leader who offers a form of solace and assurance they need and can appreciate. Later, they respond to the not-so-gentle coercion of a group of nomadic sun-worshippers to follow their political and spiritual path. The whole mood of the book is one of the continuing decline of the human condition, as though the characters were lingering leftovers from the cataclysmic war, waiting to lose either their humanity or their lives.

80. Sheckley, Robert. *Journey beyond Tomorrow*. London: Gollancz, 1964. 188 pp. Other Edition: London: Gollancz, 1969, 189 pp, ISBN 575003510.

When humor occurs at all in future war literature, its form is most often satire. Sheckley sustains an entertaining satirical point of view throughout this apparently simple story of Joeness, a young American from Polynesia who makes his first and only visit to civilization in the twenty-first century. Joeness first travels to the United States, his parents' homeland, and is caught up with the beatniks, the legal system, truck drivers, a crazy house, a university, and a utopian community. His naiveté and honesty are never quite dispelled, but he learns to be wary. When Joeness is drafted for government service and sent to Russia as an emissary, his returning plane accidentally sets off highly automated American missile defenses. Machine failure and human error compound to escalate this incident to a missile war that destroys America and most of Europe and Asia. Joeness manages to sail back to Polynesia where he lives to become a very old man.

81. Tabori, Paul. *The Survivors*. London: World Distributors, 1964. 170 pp.

At the end of this remarkable book, the main character, an American newsman and sometime spy, congratulates himself on surviving. That is no small feat. In Europe of the immediate future, he lives through several wars and much radical governmental change. The first war is a farce. The Russians invade Britain with a new gas that induces passiveness and good humor in everyone, including their own troops, who refuse to fight. Later, Scandinavians and Arabs attack the imaginary Balkan nation of Viganola. Still later, the Arabs attack Britain with nuclear and chemical weapons. This leads to a general European war in which at least one-seventh of the population is killed. When this last war ends through the exhaustion of most participants, many of the surviving nations form monarchies. These events are tied together through the American reporter, who is somehow present for them all. In addition to the rather active plot, the book features a satirical style that is often funny despite the awful events it conveys.

1965

82. Ball, Florence E. *Zero Plus Ten*. New York: Exposition Press, 1965. 131 pp.

Persons familiar with the Colorado mountains will doubt this story of primitive survival after a nuclear war in 1964. On a trip away from civilization, two newlyweds find themselves stranded in the mountains north of Denver when the bombs fall. With no tools or equipment except what they scavenge from a car, they manage to survive and to establish an isolated but adequate lifestyle. Later in the book, a baby girl is born and the wife dies. Eventually, the father and daughter make contact with a community in North Park, Colorado, and learn that nobody has any idea of the origins or the outcome of the war. Unrealistic dialog and an impossible plot are not helped by simple line drawings of such subjects as a hut in the forest. In all, the book seems to have no point.

83. Braddon, Russell, *The Year of the Angry Rabbit*. New York: Norton, 1965. 181 pp. LC 65-18017.

Satire and sadness combine in this effective story of Australian biological warfare at the end of the twentieth century. Australian scientists, working to poison a growing population of rabbits, develop a biological agent that is instantly fatal to humans. An opportunistic Australian prime minister has vials of the poison planted around the world, which can be activated by remote control. He then blackmails all world governments to disarm. As object lessons, he kills all the participants in a black versus white civil war in Rhodesia and the crews of a Sino-Japanese invasion fleet heading toward Australia. He later forces all warring nations to conduct limited and controlled wars in the Australian Outback. Nuclear physicists are exiled to the Falkland Islands. After some years of Australian world domination, scientists learn of a strain of huge, mutant rabbits that resulted from the poisoning experiments and subsequent nuclear bombing. Despite all human efforts, the rabbits take over Australia, driving out the white inhabitants. After all the humans have gone, the rabbits accidentally trigger the mechanism that will release the fatal poison worldwide.

84. Dick, Philip K. *Dr. Bloodmoney*. New York: Ace Books, 1965. 290 pp. Other Editions: New York: Dell, 1980, 304 pp, ISBN 0440114896; Boston: Gregg, 1977, 222 pp, LC 77-4508.

Dick's world of 1981 is distorted enough even before the novel's thermonuclear war. Afterwards, survivors around the San Francisco

Bay area must cope with mutant animals, plants, and humans as well as a reduced level of civilization. Social, economic, and family relationships are bizarre, as are many of the individual characters. They include a male child living inside his sister's abdomen, a black television salesman, and a phocomelus—the limbless child of a mother who took thalidomide in the 1960s. Except for a brief mention of a national military government in Cheyenne and other occasional references to survivors elsewhere in the country, there is no sense of how the world outside of the Bay Area has organized itself after the war. There is, however, a clear indication that the future will be every bit as weird as the immediate postwar period. Despite its utter strangeness and outwardly depressing subject, this is a credible literary effort that is interesting to read.

85. George, Peter. *Commander-1*. New York: Delacorte Press, 1965. 254 pp. LC 65-24932. Other Editions: New York: Dell, 1965, 251 pp; London: Heinemann, 1965, 252 pp.

George attempts too much with this complicated novel, but the several related stories merge for an effective impact. Most important is the account of a plot by the Chinese to trick the Soviet Union and the U.S. into a mutually destructive nuclear war by the detonation of carefully placed suitcase bombs. The Chinese are successful on Christmas 1965, but the holocaust they unleash is worldwide. After initial exchanges of nuclear weapons, the remnants of nations that survive are attacked by other remnants with biological substances. World population is reduced to less than one million. The second story is about the emergence of a military dictatorship in America after the war. A submarine commander returns to one of several safe bases that had secretly been prepared before the war. He subdues the civilian leadership and selects a few thousand of the best physical and psychological specimens among the refugees for chemical and hypnotic indoctrination. Then he transports his military staff and colonists to another secure reserve sanctuary on a Pacific island. After dealing with a few dissenters who object to military dictatorship, the commander is free to plan the reconquest of the scattered human groups that remain alive on the planet.

86. Hersey, John. *White Lotus*. New York: Knopf, 1965. 683 pp. LC 65-1104. Other Editions: New York: Bantam, 1966, 691 pp, ISBN 0553-022679; New York: Knopf, 1976, 683 pp, LC 65-11104.

This allegory of the universal slave experience is long and painfully tedious. White Lotus, an American girl, lives in her village in Arizona in the New Era, some time after America's defeat in the Yellow War. She and others are captured by American slavers and sold to China, where a revived imperial government rules. The white slaves in China attempt to better their lot through a form of passive resistance that involves standing on one leg in the "sleeping bird" stance. The nature of the whites' servitude and their relationships with their Chinese masters are described and analyzed in exhaustive detail. There are many lengthy reflections on the nature of slavery and servitude. Hersey writes convincingly about Chinese scenes, and to some extent his prose is similar to translations of Chinese stories in English. However, the impression remains that White Lotus and her friends are as much buried in their situation as the story is buried in a mass of words.

87. Kraslow, David and Boyd, Robert S. *A Certain Evil*. Boston: Little, Brown, 1965. 346 pp. LC 65-10898.

To a bibliographer working in 1984, when the United States is involved with revolutionary and counterrevolutionary forces in at least two Latin American countries, this novel is particularly evocative. The imaginary republic of Navidad has all the classic elements of political turmoil, including an authoritarian government, communist revolutionaries, idealists, spies, and politicians of every persuasion. Most of the action occurs among government and press figures in the United States as they attempt to manipulate one another and events among other people far away. Much of the dialog about the hope and futility of such manipulation reads exactly like the press reports and public pronouncements issued nearly 20 years after it was written. The war, when it comes, is a relatively minor revolution with only about 100 casualties, but the message of this competent political thriller is of some consequence if it is read and understood within the context of today's Central American policies.

1966

88. Drury, Allen. *Capable of Honor*. Garden City, NY: Doubleday, 1966. 531 pp. LC 66-20961.

This is the first future war novel in the political series that began with the author's well-known *Advise and Consent* (1959) in which imaginary wars play a significant part. In the fictional Central African nation of Gorotoland, communist rebels slaughter American missionaries and destroy Standard Oil facilities, which prompts the president of the United States to send in troops. Shortly afterward, a rebellion in Panama threatens the canal, and American forces lead a reluctant OAS contingent to attempt to restore the situation. These two wars are very much in the background of national political events in the United States. The novelist portrays liberal politicians and journalists in an exceptionally unfavorable light—they encourage and support an irresponsible and violent antiwar movement. Edward M. Jason and Orrin Knox, characters who become U.S. presidents in later books cited elsewhere in this bibliography, are introduced in a substantial way here. Although the wars are important to political events in the novel, there are no descriptions of actual fighting. In this book, as in his later ones, the author makes his biases clear in introductory material. Unfortunately, here as elsewhere, he is heavy-handed in conveying them in a fictional context.

89. McCutchan, Philip. *A Time for Survival.* London: Harrap, 1966. 207 pp. LC 67-81532.

In 1995, a revolution in Southeast Asia brings war between America and China. Soon the entire world is involved. In Britain, a Defence Ministry official, John Clayton, survives a Sino-Soviet nuclear attack with his wife and baby in a government shelter. They emerge from underground and wander the totally devastated landscape, eventually making contact with a small military unit and other scattered survivors. Chinese and Soviet airplanes are sighted, and soon Chinese troops appear on the ground. Some are captured, interrogated under torture, and executed by Gurkha soldiers. The British survivors see American airplanes and join with an American pilot who was shot down. From him they learn that the United States may soon launch a nuclear attack on the Sino-Soviet invaders of Britain. Despite desperate and heroic attempts to prevent the attack and to escape by sea, the survivors are destroyed by American bombs. The characters and their relationships are interesting, but plot details are sketchy, and action is not described well despite the author's clear attempt to achieve realism.

1967

90. Brunner, John. *The Jagged Orbit.* New York: Ace Books, 1967. 343 pp.

Brunner is no doubt a capable literary talent, but in this work, he employs curious and obscure devices of style, physical layout, and story line that do much to inhibit a reader. His central thesis appears to be that the United States in 2014 has inherited the racial problems that were not solved in the 1960s. There was a black revolution in the 1980s that seems to have been put down and a minor war in New Guinea. Citizens in the early twenty-first century go heavily armed, and their lives are dominated by communications media, psychotherapy, and cult religions. In the midst of the story, there is another black insurrection in New York, but its relationship to the rest of the plot is obscure. One hundred chapters, some of only a few words, add confusion to an already choppy and disorganized presentation.

91. Cordell, Alexander. *The Deadly Eurasian.* New York: Weybright & Tally, 1967. 186 pp. LC 68-28271. British Title: *The Bright Cantonese,* London: Gollancz, 1967, 224 pp, LC 67-109333.

One persuasive argument against the proliferation of nuclear weapons is that they might fall into the "wrong" hands. Cordell supposes that an American naval officer illegally releases an armed tactical nuclear rocket onto Mainland China. The weapon detonates near Canton, causing much destruction. After imaginative and implausible adventures by a female Chinese spy—the deadly Eurasian of the title—it is determined that the officer was acting in favor of big business. The idea is that a new war would mean increased profits for military industries. Even though the Chinese spy discovers that the attack on her country was not a result of official U.S. policy, she cannot prevent another agent from setting off the mechanism of revenge. This takes the form of seven suitcase atomic bombs detonated in major U.S. cities. There is no indication of the further course of hostilities after this action.

92. High, Philip E. *These Savage Futurians.* New York: Ace Books, 1967. 134 pp. Other Edition: London: Denis Dobson, 1969, 134 pp, ISBN 234772921.

In this novel, the wars that destroyed most of the world in the 1980s were small affairs; there was no major nuclear exchange. Economic and political deterioration had begun decades before, and humans had lost their will. At the beginning of the twenty-second century, two bands of scientists, both descendants of groups that had hidden in shelters, struggle for domination of the remaining population. There is a masterful and imaginative display of future technology, including an artificial island in the Atlantic Ocean that serves as headquarters for the scientists who represent evil, and a huge underground laboratory in Britain where the good scientists do their work. Among the latter group is a genius in the field of microengineering. A minor subplot about a tiny, nonhuman race takes this book technically out of the scope of this bibliography, but these beings appear briefly on the periphery of the story and depart without having affected much. A rapprochement among the two human groups leaves good triumphant over evil and promises that the remainder of the world's population will be raised up from savagery.

93. Pangborn, Edgar. *The Judgment of Eve*. New York: Dell, 1967. 159 pp. Other Editions: London: Rapp & Whiting, 1968, 189 pp; New York: Avon, 1976, 159 pp, ISBN 030007576.

A love story set among the survivors of nuclear war amounts to a certain expression of hope. Around 1970, a one-day war occurred in which a few American cities were hit, but the country was depopulated by the plagues that followed. The story begins some 25 years later in New England where a few small settlements struggle to grow—some people are sterile and others produce mutants. Eve, a woman of 28, lives with her blind mother on an isolated farm. She is courted by three suitors who visit her, then journey independently for a few months, and finally return so that she can select one as a mate. The suitors' travels bring them into contact with individuals and groups who have made different and sometimes tortured adjustments to the postwar world. Civilization is generally at the level of the mid-nineteenth century, centered around hunting and farming. The love story ends happily but vaguely, and the characters are left in a pastoral setting with abundant opportunity.

94. Sutton, Jeff. *H-Bomb over America*. New York: Ace Books, 1967. 190 pp.

Sutton combines two specific and different ideas about future war in this ambitious adventure novel. He first addresses the common fear that a madman or fanatic might obtain nuclear weapons. Specifically, a Soviet officer, under Chinese influence, takes over a missile base in 1973 and puts a nuclear bomb in orbit over the U.S. The second and more comforting premise is that modern wars might be fought by a few specialists—perhaps with machines in space—rather than being imposed on civilian populations. This technical conception is handled with energy and imagination. Satellites, space stations, and the other machines of this decade are predicted with considerable accuracy. Characterization and plotting are less impressive. While the world waits on the edge of nuclear war, Russia and the U.S. stab at each other in relatively minor ways: machines fight men in space, there is a battle between submarines in the North Pacific, and the rebel Russian base is destroyed by a U.S. missile. In the end, general war is avoided. The characters who perform all this action are too numerous and difficult to distinguish from one another. The author is not always able to sustain the tension he seeks, and the main story is weakened by too many subplots.

1968

95. Dick, Philip K. *Do Androids Dream of Electric Sheep?* Garden City, NY: Doubleday, 1968. 210 pp. LC 68-11779. Other Editions: New York: New American Library, 1969, 159 pp; London: Granada, 1972, 183 pp, ISBN 0586036059; Other Title: *Blade Runner (Do Androids Dream of Electric Sheep?)*, New York: Ballantine, 1982, 216 pp.

Like its title, the book asks more questions than it provides answers. In 1999, the world is polluted with radioactive dust from World War Terminus. Nobody remembers who began the war or who won it. Its legacy is not victory or defeat in a classic military sense, but the gradual decay of life forms and the degradation of human intelligence and society. To encourage migration to other planets, the government offers colonists android slaves—civilian versions of the Synthetic Freedom Fighter developed during the war. When six advanced androids escape from a colony and return to earth, they are chased and destroyed by a specialized bounty hunter in the ruins of the San Francisco area. The central problem for all the characters, including the androids, is to understand what is real; what is actually alive; and what species or machines should survive. The author offers substantial philosophical points without becoming tendentious. The 1982 motion picture *Blade Runner* was loosely based on this novel.

96. Drury, Allen. *Preserve and Protect*. Garden City, NY: Doubleday, 1968. 394 pp. LC 68-26725.

Elsewhere in this bibliography, other books in Drury's series of Washington political novels are cited (see entries 88, 124, and 137). The brush fire wars in Panama and in the imaginary African nation of Gorotoland are features in this book, too. As in the others, they are background events, important only because of their effect on American politics. As American forces achieve some gains on the battle fronts, antiwar activities in the U.S. take on a more aggressive and much nastier aspect. The parallel to Vietnam is obvious. Drury's aggregation of conservative heros and liberal villains talk their way verbosely through this story no differently from the others. At the end, neither the wars nor the internal American political divisions caused by them are resolved. The special virtue of *Preserve and Protect* is that it is slightly shorter than other books in the series.

97. Fennerton, William. *The Lucifer Cell*. New York: Atheneum, 1968. 306 pp. LC 68-12537. Other Edition: London: Hodder & Stoughton, 1968, 306 pp.

Fennerton places his novel in 1978. The Chinese communists have won a major war and occupy Russia and Western Europe. At one point in the war, America has used atomic weapons in unpopulated areas as demonstrations of power, but the Chinese have not been deterred. In England, the Chinese military government operates through a puppet prime minister and cabinet. The story deals with an operative in the British resistance, called the Home Army, who leads a team to assassinate the prime minister. Their work is completed in the totalitarian and depressed environment of England. In the background, there are rumors that American, African, and Australian forces are organizing themselves for a major attack on the Chinese homeland, but these events are still pending when the book ends. Fennerton writes fluently, and his underground characters are suitably suspicious and world-weary.

98. Hay, John. *The Invasion*. London: Hodder and Stoughton, 1968. 192 pp. LC 76-419170.

In the near future, there is a general and destructive world nuclear war. As part of it, forces of the South East Asian Republic—a combination of Malaysia and Indonesia—invade and occupy Australia. The troops at a rural sheep and cattle station include both Chinese and Malay individuals. Through crises engineered by the station's former owner, the two national groups fight each other with devastating results. Soon afterward, the remainder are killed in a flood. Within a month, the few survivors gain the impression that the occupation government of Australia has either disappeared or forgotten about them. The characters, who include whites, Asians, and aborigines, face the future of a primitive subsistence life on their own. Although it moves fast, this novel takes an interesting look at the world views of individuals of different racial and cultural backgrounds.

99. Leiber, Fritz. *A Specter Is Haunting Texas*. New York: Wilder, 1968. 250 pp.

This book might be called an overdone parody of Texan exuberance. There is certainly no light touch in this story of Texas 250 years after a nuclear war has destroyed much of the rest of the world. When it is visited by a moon colonist, Greater Texas has assumed control of most of North America. Russian and the Pacific Black Republic occupy the remainder of the globe. Hormones have made Texans huge, while their slaves are tiny Mexicans kept humble with medical implants and drugs. Characters and actions are complicated, grandiose, and intended to be humorous. The moon colonist falls in with a conspiracy by Mexicans to overthrow the Texas government. His numerous adventures are recounted in detail, especially those in areas that bear physical scars from World War III. The revolution is finally successful, and the new nation that emerges afterwards is more in the image of the former United States. Leiber's pace is frantic, and the inventions never cease. While it is original in concept, this novel outpaces even the most diligent reader.

1969

100. Alter, Robert Edmond. *Path to Savagery*. New York: Avon, 1969. 174 pp.

The title seems inappropriate for what is, in the context of future war literature, a pleasant and hopeful story. Sometime after the beginning of the twenty-first century, America has degenerated to savagery after a nuclear war 20 years earlier. Falk, the hero, is a loner who wanders generally northward in search of a rumored new settlement called Genesis. With the help of his considerable wit and a submachine gun, he avoids packs of destructive Neanderthalers and falls in temporarily with a group of Flockers whose abode is a flooded department store.

Falk works through a nasty dispute with the Flocker leader over the latter's woman, kills him, and resumes his northward journey. His companion is a woman of harsh antecedents. In addition to credentials as a survivor, she has an apparently honest affection for Falk and a bag of hand grenades. The reader is left with the feeling, and indeed the hope, that Genesis might exist and that the couple will find it. Characters are quite realistic, and the action is vivid in this excellent story.

101. Corley, Edwin. *Siege*. New York: Stein & Day, 1969. 384 pp. LC 69-17948.

Taking place in the immediate future, this novel is a period piece of the 1960s. The story of black revolution offers a balanced and rational view of the racial tensions in the United States at that time. Much of this emerges in accounts of the background of the revolution's military commander, Shawcross, and the political commissar, Gray. Historical events, including the assassination of Malcolm X, are worked into the story. The blacks create a secret army and use it to take over New York City, which they hold in ransom for New Jersey—the proposed independent black state. Several African governments recognize the insurrection. Counterattacks by police and military units fare badly. Ultimately, the city is set on fire and the black military commander surrenders before he is killed. One of the best aspects of the book is its portrayal of the dilemma of loyal black soldiers.

102. Garbo, Norman. *The Movement*. New York: William Morrow, 1969. 407 pp. LC 78-3692. Other Edition: London: Michael Joseph, 1970, 416 pp.

Comparisons to Kent State are obvious in this novel of student violence in 1971, and the future is predicted with sad accuracy. At imaginary Chadwick University in Michigan, the largest academic institution in the country, a militant student organization called The Movement takes over the campus. Confrontation and violence escalate until the National Guard is called in to recover the campus. Guard tactics are imprudent, and an entire brigade, with armored vehicles, is captured intact. Now superbly equipped, the students are nonetheless unable to resist regular airborne and helicopter forces that finally defeat them. The central story has to do with youthful social ideas gone out of control. It is a timely subject, but the author does not have the credible position of an insider. Midwestern university students in the 1960s and early 1970s were a more diverse group than Garbo represents them to be, and National Guard officers were not so timid.

103. Holm, Sven. *Termush*. London: Faber & Faber, 1969. 110 pp. LC 71-480331.

This small but carefully written book is an exploration of the morality of the fallout shelter. Termush is the name of a survivalist estate and hotel where privileged persons of an unnamed country have retreated after a nuclear war. The narrator describes his own ambiguous feelings and actions as people from the outside try with increasing success to breach Termush's defenses. The management and medical staff of Termush try to make some accommodation, but in the end, the pressure from the outside is too great, and the paying guests of Termush abandon it by sea. The final impression conveyed is that the future of even these survivors will be short, for they all seem affected by radiation.

104. Reed, Kit. *Armed Camps*. London: Faber & Faber, 1969. 176 pp. ISBN 571091X.

This British writer makes a confused and unpleasant prediction about the future of life in America. There are two separate stories in the novel, and they almost come together at the end. Until then, anything that is understood about the book must be extracted from a most confusing arrangement of words. It is sometime in the late twentieth century, and there is considerable civil disorder. A girl from this environment falls in with the members of a utopian colony that is ultimately destroyed by government forces. In a parallel story, a professional army officer participates in the ritualized single combat that has replaced international wars. Both of these characters wonder at great length about the meaning of their lives. The officer disobeys an impossible order and is assigned to a lifetime punishment from which the girl from the utopian community might rescue him. America, however, is a very ugly place in Reed's mind, and there is really little hope for either character.

1970–1979

105. Aldiss, Brian W. *Barefoot in the Head*. Garden City, NY: Double-day, 1970. 281 pp. LC 74-97644.

The book's subtitle "A European Fantasia" certainly fits the tone of this story. The Acid Head War began when millionaire Kuwaiti pilots attacked Europe with psycho-chemical aerosol bombs. The psychedelic drug the bombs contained was undetectable, and its after-effects could last a lifetime. Aldiss presents a Europe after this war in which human thought and communication have been permanently altered by this unique weapon. His hero is Charteris, a Serbian wanderer who ultimately becomes a sort of Messiah in postwar Europe. The distinctive literary style includes many poems as part of the narrative and the invention and alteration of numerous words. This extraordinary presentation clouds a reader's initial understanding of setting, plot, action, and characters, but the concept of chemical warfare involving psychedelics is fascinating.

106. Carter, Angela. *Heroes and Villains*. New York: Simon & Schuster, 1970. 214 pp. LC 75-116501. Other Edition: New York: Pocket Books, 1972, 176 pp.

A romantic fantasy set in the aftermath of future nuclear war has obstacles to overcome if the plot is to make sense in the setting. This one is at least consistent internally. It is a graphic and disturbing story with ugly incidents throughout. Some three generations after a nuclear war, descendants of the survivors live in groups that have little regular contact with one another. Professors, protected in their compounds by soldiers, preserve the old knowledge. Tribes of barbarians roam through the forests and ruins of North America, using both bows and primitive firearms in occasional battles against horrible mutants called

Out People. There is no central government or any national economic system. The female protagonist, Marianne, flees a Professor compound to follow a barbarian lover. His rape of her is one of many brutal, bizarre acts. Others include murder and flogging as the tribe migrates slowly toward the sea. There is, however, no cleansing in either a hygenic or symbolic sense when they finally arrive. There may be some hope that life will go on, but there is small chance that it will improve.

107. Egleton, Clive. *A Piece of Resistance*. New York: Coward-McCann, 1970. 252 pp. LC 79-96786. Other Edition: Los Angeles: Pinnacle, 1974, 248 pp, ISBN 0523405634.

Few Russian characters appear and even fewer speak in this adventure about resistance fighters in a near-future Britain occupied by the Soviets. The brutal occupation has followed a brief war, and the English people are divided into collaborators and the resistance. Garnett, one of the few professional army officers to survive wholesale slaughter, leads a raid on a Soviet prison to free an important member of the resistance. The raid is a costly failure, and afterwards, Garnett loses what little faith he has in the resistance command. In its own context, this fast-paced story is believable, and the author, a serving officer, supplies abundant details about weapons and military hardware. His picture of occupied Britain is an interesting mix of traditional democratic institutions and values altered to conform to a crushing Soviet occupation.

108. Goulart, Ron. *After Things Fell Apart*. New York: Ace Books, 1970. 189 pp. Other Edition: Boston: Gregg, 1977, 189 pp, ISBN 0839823681.

The title is perfectly descriptive. Near the end of the twentieth century, the United States has broken into numerous small tribes, nations, enclaves, and city-states. Many of them engage in permanent, low-level war with one another. A failed Chinese invasion of Southern California in the 1980s or 1990s hastened the demise of the central government and political order. The results are the chaotic and bizarre conditions described in the book. The story deals with a private detective who tries to identify and stop a group of feminist commandos who plan to assassinate the leaders of San Francisco and take over that independent enclave. The detective's adventures bring him into contact with persons and groups who represent twentieth-century ideas carried to extremes. Early in the book, for instance, a group of muzzle-loading rifle enthusiasts battle black militants for control of the Golden Gate Bridge. Some of the humor is effective, and the vision of the future as reflected by the title is more crazy than ugly.

109. Lightener, A. M. *The Day of the Drones*. New York: Bantam, 1970. 213 pp.

In Africa, a peaceful and thoughtful people live with the knowledge that their elementary science and scholarship are remnants of a higher culture destroyed by a war among white men some five centuries before. The narrator is a young woman who studies literature and reads the surviving fragments of Shakespeare. She and a few others are sent on a journey of discovery to the north in the only operating airplane. They pass over devastated territories, barren of humans and mammals, to land finally in England. There, they find a very primitive tribe whose society is copied from that of bees. Women capable of producing large numbers of nonmutant offspring achieve high status, while men are used for breeding, then killed. Bees have grown to the size of birds, and the English keep them as domestic animals. This first attempt at international relations in 500 years produces mixed results. As the book ends, the explorers are back in Africa with a complete copy of the works of Shakespeare among their meagre loot, and any future exploration seems doubtful.

110. Mano, D. Keith. *War Is Heaven*. Garden City, NY: Doubleday, 1970. 226 pp. LC 75-97611.

Published during the height of American involvement in Vietnam, *War Is Heaven* might well be a script for military adventures in Latin America 13 years later. A group of U.S. advisers helps government troops in the imaginary nation of Camaguay fight a communist insurgency. The war is a classic affair of jungle patrolling, ambushes, and futile efforts to instill military professionalism into indigenous troops. The characters include a competent, thoughtful sergeant, some inexperienced young soldiers, an alienated black, and a careerist senior officer. Mano deals competently and familiarly with the effect of a futile war on men's relationships and values. Military specifics are presented with refreshing accuracy, and the realistic style is appropriate for the subject. War is not heaven, of course, and Mano lets the reader know it. Camaguay might be a Spanish Vietnam, or it could reflect today's problems in El Salvador.

111. Tucker, Wilson. *The Year of the Quiet Sun*. New York: Ace Books, 1970. 252 pp.

Time travel is technically outside the scope of this bibliography, but it is used here to provide access to a continued state of future war from the late 1970s through 2000 A.D. In 1978, Israel is at war and the U.S. is still involved in the Vietnamese conflict. A social scientist is brought into a U.S. government time-travel experiment. As he and several colleagues visit the future several times up to the twenty-first century, they find a continually worsening situation. In 1980, the Vietnam War has expanded into a general Asian land war involving 2,000,000 Americans. By 1999, some 12,000,000 American troops are lost overseas, and a racial civil war rages for nearly two years. The Chinese side with American black revolutionaries and attack Chicago and other American cities with nuclear weapons. Near the end, the Constitution is suspended, and a dictatorial president is assassinated. Then the whole country is left in ruins and anarchy. There appears to be no invasion in the offing, for by the beginning of the twenty-first century, the entire world is depopulated and exhausted. That all this is readable, even interesting, is a tribute to Tucker's ability to write science fiction.

1971

112. Donis, Miles. *The Fall of New York*. New York: David McKay Company, 1971. 216 pp. LC 71-149091.

In this novel, the United States is in political and economic chaos. Nothing works anymore. A continuation of the Vietnam War combined with racial divisions and ecological destruction tear the nation apart. A revolt within the armed forces has involved military action on a large scale, and the civilian government has fled to Portugal. In most of the countryside, armed bands and regional militia battle for control against an alliance of the Army and the Mafia. In New York, most of the adults have fled and packs of teenagers roam the city scavenging the ruins. Donis describes the dead city well, and his juveniles of the future are especially delinquent. His theme deals with the abandonment of one generation by another and the abandonment by a whole people of their heritage. These larger issues are not in the minds of the soldiers, who finally surround the city and move in to incorporate it into the new military American state.

113. Egleton, Clive. *Last Post for a Partisan*. New York: Pinnacle, 1971.
224 pp. ISBN 0523003447. Other Editions: London: Hodder & Stoughton,
1971, 224 pp, LC 72-26796; New York: Coward, McCann & Geohegan,
1971, 224 pp, LC 71-136447.

Garnett is a former British officer who served in the forces that were
defeated by the Soviets when they invaded Britain five years before
the story opens. At present, Garnett is an operative of the Resistance,
and this novel deals with his work against double agents in the
provinces. Although the Soviet occupation is in place, Russian characters are absent. Garnett is a typically alienated spy-hero; the man
with the past too brutal to describe and with unspoken convictions
perhaps too vague to articulate. His enemies, as he works through the
convoluted relationships of spies and terrorists, are other Englishmen.
They include the collaborationist authorities, who serve the Soviets, as
well as traitors within the Resistance. This active adventure story has
abundant details about weapons and automobiles, but there is no sense
of how the events of the characters' lives fit into any larger pattern of
postwar Britain. Also, except in an epilogue, there is no picture of the
form and practices of the Soviet occupation.

114. Harrison, M. John. *The Committed Men*. Garden City, NY: Doubleday, 1971. 183 pp. LC 70-157597. Other Edition: London: New Authors,
1971, 184 pp.

Harrison places his story in England at a time soon enough after a
military disaster that living persons still remember it. There have been
internecine wars, and military struggles continue among regional
governments and bands of mercenaries who have fallen heir to the
power abandoned by national authorities. The countryside is disorganized and falling apart. The people are sickly, scabrous, cancerous,
and weak. Four wanderers, an elderly man who had been a doctor, a
woman, a young cripple, and a mutant dwarf accidentally come
together and gain possession of an infant who is clearly one of a new
and completely different species. Although generally human in ap-
pearance, the baby has a tough, radiation-resistant skin. Following
rumors, the party travels south to find what they hope to be a tribe of
creatures like the baby. In an era of hopelessness and savagery, their
commitment to the child becomes the central drive of all their lives. In
the ruined country, they encounter human groups who try to kill the
child. The humans are a dying species, and the mutants are the hope
for the future.

115. Lange, Oliver. *Vandenberg*. New York: Stein & Day, 1971. 333 pp. LC 77-144774. Other Editions: London: Peter Davies, 1971, 333 pp, ISBN 432085602; New York: Bantam, 1972, 345 pp; London: Panther, 1980, 352 pp, ISBN 586048820.

The conflict in this novel can be expressed on one level as "cowboys versus Russians." In the near future, the Soviets have successfully invaded the U.S. using germ warfare rather than nuclear weapons. They install a moderate military government that allows many American social and economic institutions to continue in recognizable form. The title character is Eugene Vandenberg of New Mexico, a painter and rancher in his 50s, who is given to reflection and writing about the decline of America. Sections of his "journal" appear throughout the book. After an escalating feud with Soviet authorities, Vandenberg and a group of classic Southwestern types, including Spanish-Americans, launch an attack on a detention facility. Most are killed by aircraft during a retreat. The romantic and idealistic concepts of the American West are no match for modern aircraft. Sensitive and well written, this novel manages to convey fatalism without overwhelming gloom.

116. Pendleton, Don. *Civil War II*. New York: Pinnacle, 1971. 249 pp. ISBN 0523007582.

The Negro revolt of 1999 emerges from the systematic oppression of blacks by whites during the preceding 30 years. The races are entirely separate. Whites have moved to new strip cities to work in an efficient system of automated agriculture while most blacks remain on welfare in the hulks of large cities. Other blacks predominate in the civil service and the military. They are thus able to control the armed forces and stage a successful, rapid coup d'etat. In physical control of a cowed white population, the black leader installs a trusted white man as head of a provisional government. He is able to resist a threatened invasion from starving China, but a widespread rampage of black forces in the South represents a greater danger. Finally, the director of the provisional government detonates tactical nuclear weapons over the area and threatens the immediate use of more against rebellious black troops. This action quells the rebellion, and the country successfully goes about a reconciliation of the races. This is an interesting idea written as a political thriller.

1972

117. Breggin, Roger Peter. *After the Good War*. New York: Stein & Day, 1972. 235 pp. LC 72-80334.

In 2212, America is a totalitarian, pleasure-loving state whose citizens are discouraged from productive work or original thought. Romantic and family love have been replaced by sensual pleasure and frequent sex. The Good War appears to have been fought and won at the end of the twentieth century by means that are not given in detail. Other minor wars have occurred between Israel and the Arabs and among blacks and whites in the United States. Racial prejudice and anti-Semitism have eliminated blacks and Jews from American society. In this environment, two lovers, Gambol and Rogar, seek an emotional relationship that is outside of approved bounds. In the end, they steal an aircraft and escape to Israel. All this is conveyed in an obscure, unclear, and artificially stylized prose that serves to conceal rather than tell the story.

118. Cook, Glen. *The Heirs of Babylon*. New York: Signet, 1972. 192 pp.

In 2193 A.D., the remaining inhabitants of Europe prosecute a war that has gone on with little respite since the twentieth century. Sailors are directed by a shadowy High Command to sail against Australia in salvaged World War II-era warships. Much of the world, including the United States, is a radioactive wasteland, and many sailors are dubious about the need for continual war. Some crews mutiny at Gibraltar, but 200 European ships proceed to the Indian Ocean where they meet the Australian fleet in a major battle. In addition to the rickety technology of twentieth-century conventional war, the Europeans employ another relic—an atomic bomb. The officers of one ship attempt to leave the battle, but only a few survivors make it to the Indian mainland where they contemplate the long walk home. One has the sense that nothing was learned about the futility of war and that the future holds more pointless battles.

119. Egleton, Clive. *The Judas Mandate*. New York: Coward, McCann & Geohegan, 1972. 251 pp. LC 78-183550. Other Editions: London: Hodder & Stoughton, 1972, 224 pp, ISBN 0340156600; New York: Pinnacle, 1974, 251 pp, ISBN 0523003528.

In this third and last book by Egleton about Soviet-occupied Britain (see entries 107 and 113), Russian characters are as scarce as ever, and there is still no comprehensive idea of daily life under Soviet occupation. Normal British social and commercial institutions are still operating, and there remains some sense of class differences. The Soviets have become involved in a war with China and have reduced their occupation forces to three divisions. Members of the resistance movement as well as officials of the collaborationist government are seeking an accommodation with the Soviets that will restore a completely British government. Garnett, Egleton's hardened hero, engineers the complicated rescue of six political prisoners destined for transport to Russia. In the course of the adventure, he once again loses his girlfriend. Their relationship in all three books is as brutal as the rest of the story. When a British government is finally installed, Garnett cannot give up the dangerous life and accept the compromises required to live within the Soviet area of influence.

120. Merle, Robert. *Malevil.* New York: Simon & Schuster, 1972. 575 pp. Other Editions: New York: Warner Communication Co., 1975, 590 pp, LC 73-11463; London: Michael Joseph, 1974, ISBN 0718112350.

The marvelously evocative title is the name of a castle in rural France where survivors of a 1977 nuclear war base themselves and work out their future. Like characters in similar American novels, the people who make it through the war bring with them a number of useful skills, but their European character and circumstances offer entertaining contrasts. Religion, too, plays a role here that is uniquely European. The French survivors settle into jobs as full-time farmers and part-time infantrymen. Although they are not nearly as well armed as Americans might be, their stone castle is a superb fortress that successfully resists an attack by a force that employs a modern rocket launcher. Requirements of the situation lead to an authoritarian but benevolent social system, and except for some leftover modern tools, the Middle Ages are set to begin again. Significantly, the first product of primitive industry is a system to manufacture gunpowder and to reload ammunition in the most common caliber. An able and idiomatic translation enhances a work of high quality.

121. Priest, Christopher. *Darkening Island.* New York: Harper & Row, 1972. 147 pp. LC 71-181660. British Title: *Fugue for a Darkening Island.* London: Faber & Faber, 1972, 147 pp, ISBN 0571097944.

A nuclear war has devastated Africa, and black refugees have dispersed throughout the world. In England, the African immigrants,

Afrims, are too many for the weak economy. After an unfriendly welcome, they obtain arms from abroad and precipitate an undeclared civil war that also includes royalist troops and forces from the new right-wing government. In a declining political and social situation, a man, his wife, and daughter join an increasing number of refugees. The man is thoughtful but not especially able to deal with the confused and anomalous conditions. His small family seems to bounce from one pointless confrontation to another as they encounter troops from most elements in the civil war as well as U.S. Marines and U.N. officials. The women are eventually stolen by African soldiers. When the husband discovers their bodies, he sets out on a mission of revenge. This last act provides much needed focus to a plot that is otherwise little more than an aggregation of incidents.

1973

122. Cooper, Edmund. *The Cloud Walker*. New York: Ballantine, 1973. 216 pp. Other Editions: London: Hodder & Stoughton, 1973, 223 pp, LC 74-150306; London: Coronet, 1975, 223 pp, ISBN 0340194782.

Some centuries in the future, England is again in a medieval condition. Two previous technological cultures have destroyed themselves, at least one through a missile war. Now, the official Luddite Church has replaced Christianity with its doctrine of antiknowledge. A young man, Kieron, leads his fellow inhabitants of Sussex into a new industrial and technological age. Kieron is notable for his singlemindedness as well as his intellect. Many of the other characters and events in the novel are drawn from history with a rather heavy hand. Flight is the central means of achieving Kieron's revolution. The author's enthusiasm for it puts a short and simple book rather out of balance. Characters and dialog—indeed the entire novel—are by no means convincing. However, as a parable of a rebirth of science, *The Cloud Walker* has both charm and internal consistency.

123. Cordell, Alexander. *If You Believe the Soldiers*. London: Houghton & Stoughton, 1973. 224 pp. Other Editions: New York: Doubleday, 1974, 216 pp, LC 73-13277.

The military revolt in the near future that delivers Britain into the hands of a dictator is a straightforward affair of infantry against a befuddled civilian population. Its background is economic debilitation, resentment over class distinctions, and a generally leftward political drift. The methods and processes used by ruthless soldiers to take over a legal civilian government are reminiscent of those used by the Nazi Party in Germany after 1933, and some of the personalities are similar. Particular villains are the elite Special Air Service commandoes, cast here as brutal tools of fascist oppression. This revolt occurs against a background of a world situation that includes the military destruction of Israel by Russo-Arab troops and the successful conquest of India by China. The British fascists are successful in seizing control, but they fail to mobilize and indoctrinate the populace. Instead, they victimize and alienate the middle and lower classes, and these groups provide fighters for a bloody and victorious counterrevolution. The new Worker's Democracy is in turn overthrown by a coalition of European nations, but that is only a passing event in a continually changing national situation.

124. Drury, Allen. *Come Nineveh, Come Tyre*. Garden City, NY: Doubleday, 1973. 481 pp. LC 73-9347. Other Edition: New York: Avon, 1974, 544 pp.

In a story carried forward from earlier novels (see entries 88, 96, and 137), liberal and antiwar sentiment in the U.S. leads to the election of a weak and indecisive president, Edward M. Jason. He inherits wars in Panama and in the imaginary Central African nation of Gorotoland where American troops are in combat against communist forces. Jason attempts to withdraw Americans from both nations, but the retreating troops are massacred by communist forces. The survivors are removed to captivity in the Soviet Union. Using a fishing dispute as an excuse, the Russians temporarily occupy cities in Alaska and mine the Bering Sea. On a visit to Moscow, Jason is bluntly informed of the details of Soviet worldwide military superiority. At home, political freedoms are restricted with new laws, and traditional social institutions are degraded. At the end, the U.S. is completely under Soviet domination and virtually occupied by their armed forces. Despite the importance of military events to the story, they are described only in general terms. The emphasis is on politicians in Washington, DC.

125. FitzGibbon, Constantine. *When the Kissing Had to Stop*. New Rochelle, NY: Arlington House, 1973. LC 72-88593.

This able and engrossing story of a Russian takeover of Britain in the 1960s provides an imaginative war novel. A minor, indecisive war between the U.S. and China plays a part in Soviet plans. Later, Soviet troops "invited" by an extreme left-wing British government battle resistance fighters. Essentially, however, this is a political novel written in the context of British public affairs in the early 1960s. FitzGibbon's basic message seems to be a warning about the irresponsible and idealistic excesses of the political left. His characters include sincere British patriots and leftist dupes of the Soviet Union. The plot moves swiftly as the European antinuclear movement comes to dominate British politics. FitzGibbon is a capable novelist who can create convincing characters and cause them to react to plausible situations with natural-sounding thoughts and conversations. An additional introduction and epilogue in the 1973 edition further express the author's ideas about more recent British politics, but neither adds much to an already good piece of fiction.

126. Synder, Guy. *Testament XXI*. New York: Daw Books, 1973. 144 pp. Like its characters, the reader of *Testament XXI* is caught up immediately in a severe and convoluted little world. Action occurs in an underground shelter-city near what was Madison, Wisconsin, some 130 years before. Although they are ruled by a priest-ridden monarchy, the inhabitants are aware that they are fortunate and almost alone. The world outside is a radioactive desert, suitable only for battle with the forces of Chicago, another surviving shelter-city. Personalities loom large in the pressured underground world, as men fight each other with machines whose capacities are awesome but vague. Equally unclear is the background of the entire situation and of the main character, a recently returned astronaut. Much of the story has to do with his relationship with the king, and neither these characters nor their interaction is conveyed in a complete or interesting manner. One has the impression that this skimpy and fragmented book might have been a part of a more complete text. The setting and some of the action are certainly more potentially powerful than they appear in this published version.

1974

127. Charnas, Suzy McKee. *Walk to the End of the World*. New York: Ballantine, 1974. 214 pp. Other Edition: New York: Berkeley, 1978, 246 pp, ISBN 0425042391.

Charnas has created one of the nastiest visions of the future encountered in this bibliography. Countless generations after worldwide nuclear holocaust, men blame women for the fall of the old civilization. They hold women in contemptible bondage and arrange affairs among themselves according to an elaborate yet stupid social structure that institutionalizes narcotics and homosexuality. Holdfast, the only known human settlement, is in a coastal swamp that supplies the seaweed and hemp upon which a marginal economy is based. The characters are caught up in actions of consequence and danger, but there is no apparent central purpose or goal, and no general context in which the plot can be understood. The men of Holdfast are so limited by ritual that they cannot undertake steps toward a larger and more civilized existence. The most important female character can find hope for the future only by escaping into the unknown wilderness surrounding the settlement. A reader can certainly sympathize with her motivation to flee from such an awful environment.

128. Forsyth, Frederick. *The Dogs of War*. New York: Viking, 1974. 408 pp. LC 73-19103.

The fighting in this adventure novel qualifies as a war because the military forces of an imaginary African nation, Zangaro, are fully committed. They stand little chance against the small group of white mercenaries and trained black soldiers sent to topple the government and deliver the country into the hands of a British mining company. The mercenaries are, however, idealists. They soon install another group of Africans, modeled after the Biafrans, to run the country after the takeover. Forsyth is a popular novelist, and the book is rich in convincing detail of private mercenary ventures.

129. Gawron, Jean Mark. *An Apology for Rain*. Garden City, NY: Doubleday, 1974. 176 pp. LC 73-14046.

The story is set in American places—Manhattan, Pennsylvania, New Jersey, etc.—but there is no American government or society. Instead, there are a few characters wandering around talking nonsense to each other. A civil war takes place between the Black Leathers and a group of men without uniforms. It takes the form of isolated and unrelated battles among small groups. A general named Six Million plays some dubious role in the war, and there is one huge bomb that causes temporary blindness. Throughout, the characters ask themselves about the enemy, the action, and whether it is all reality or a dream. They are no more confused than the reader, who must also wonder why such a meaningless work was published.

130. Ionesco, Eugene. *The Hermit*. Translation by Richard Seaver. New York: Viking, 1974. 169 pp. LC 73-20944.

At some time in the near future, a clerk in a Parisian office inherits a large amount of money. He quits work, purchases an apartment in one of the southern suburbs of the city, and whiles away his time to no particular purpose. A revolution breaks out and there is fighting in the streets. One side is supported by the Turks; the other by the Lapps. The narrator barricades himself in his room for a period of time and is supplied with the necessities of life by his concierge. When he emerges at last, the fighting is over, but very little has changed. Ionesco, a well-known playwright, is a key figure in the "theater of the absurd." This novel is certainly a deliberate exercise in style, but it is interesting and readable in this translation.

131. Powe, Bruce. *The Last Days of the American Empire*. New York: St. Martin's, 1974. 326 pp. LC 73-91377. Other Edition: Toronto, Canada, Macmillan of Canada, 1974, 326 pp, LC 73-314749.

In this heavily-laden book, the words and ideas so clutter each page that it is difficult for the story to find its way through. In the midst of elaborate social commentary, the plot deals with an invasion of an immensely wealthy North America by starving hordes from Africa in the twenty-first century. In a battle between advanced but seldom-used technology and desperate, hungry men, the outcome is easy to predict. Much of the story, however, has to do with the motives and practices that brought the world from the mid-twentieth century to such a condition 100 years later. Powe sees little good in American society and even less value in its likely future. At the least, one should note his marvelous imagination and unusual sense of humor.

132. Roberts, Keith. *The Chalk Giants*. London: Hutchinson, 1974. 271 pp. LC 75-325249. Other Edition: New York: G.P. Putnam's Sons, 1975, 195 pp, LC 75-10687.

One interpretation of this novel is that it describes the rise of new civilization in Britain after a future war. The first chapter is an account of the wanderings of a mutant child who is pulled in a sort of handtruck through a desolated modern landscape by two old, idiotic women. Apparently unrelated to this initial plot, the rest of the book is a romantic fantasy based on Norse models. It tells of a society in the Dark Ages that gradually established a more organized feudal system and a monotheistic religion. The people have some vague legends about an ancient, destructive war, and there is an occasional reference to the ruins of a modern road or building. Numerous new characters are introduced throughout, and only the thinnest thread of continuity is present. As the story winds down, one king has acquired cannon and has set off to unify the unnamed islands.

133. Wahloo, Per. *The Generals*. New York: Pantheon Books, 1974. 278 pp. LC 73-18730.

The civil war on an unnamed, imaginary island is described during testimony in the court-martial of one of the participants. The war took place between the Fascists and the Reds. It lasted several months and involved conventional weapons as well as gas shells. Both sides had help from foreign nations, although none was named. In the end, the Fascists won. In the court-martial that provides a frame for the story, Fascist officers on the board are portrayed unsympathetically. The accused and much-abused Red defendant is at least an innocent idealist and at best a patriot. Just as the exhausting ritual of the trial reaches its end, a coup takes place among the members of the Fascist government. One of the leaders, who had been on the court-martial board, no longer has time to play legalistic games. He orders a subordinate to take the defendant to the basement and shoot him.

134. Waldrop, Howard, and Saunders, Jake. *The Texas-Israeli War*. New York: Ballantine, 1974. ISBN 0345277368 (A Del Rey Book). Other Edition: New York: Ballantine, 1974, ISBN 0345241827 (Ballantine/science fiction).

The world wars of the 1980s have reduced the population of the planet by 90 percent through deaths, radiation, and plague. In Alaska and Canada, Chinese invaders are still being pushed back. Texas has seceded from the Union and touched off a second American civil war. In 1999, Israeli mercenaries in a federal armored unit are sent behind Texas lines to rescue the president of the United States who has been a prisoner for nine months. Although fuel is in short supply, armor rather than infantry does most of the fighting in the war. There are almost no aircraft and some Texan units move on horseback. Laser cannons dominate the battlefield, supported by traditional artillery and small arms. The weapons and battles are described realistically, and the characters act and speak believably. The rescue and associated political intrigue add little to what is, despite its awkward title, an interesting war novel in a credible setting.

1975

135. Callenbach, Ernest. *Ecotopia*. Berkeley, CA: Banyan Tree Books, 1975. 167 pp. LC 74-84366. Other Edition: New York: Bantam, 1977, ISBN 0553104896.

Citizens in Washington, Oregon, and Northern California fought no war of independence when they seceded from the Union in 1980 to form the new nation of Ecotopia. Instead they blackmailed the United States with nuclear mines concealed in major American cities. By the time the U.S. attacked its lost territories in the Helicopter War of 1982, the Ecotopians had organized a home defense based on the Swiss model. Over 7,000 helicopters were shot down with missiles before the U.S. called off the invasion. The epistolary account of this war occurs in this novel set in 1999, based on the articles and journal of the first American newsman to visit Ecotopia for 20 years. He conveys a full description of an economic, political, and social system based on ecological and humanistic principles. Against a background of a polluted America at war with Brazil, Ecotopia appears to be a reasonable and peaceful country, although credulity would be strained for one to believe that all elements of society there fit together as nicely as the narrator claims. Nonetheless, this is an attractive vision of what might be, in which even national defense can be viewed in organic and holistic terms.

136. Clément, Francois. *Birth of an Island*. New York: Simon & Schuster, 1975. 346 pp. LC 74-19100.

Survival in paradise is a different fate from that of most characters in this genre. Clément sets his story on a small island near Tahiti, where a few French officials and about 1,000 natives survive the war that destroys most of civilization. The narration is in the form of an account written by the senior French official in his old age, and it covers approximately the first decade of postwar life. The impression conveyed is that affairs on the remote, idyllic island proceed not much differently from the way that they would have had there not been a war. Some brutal hostilities between the natives and a group of refugees remind the reader that these are primitive people. The central fact of the administrator's life is that he must deal with a foreign, less advanced culture, not that he is a survivor of a nuclear war. When the islanders build a ship and sail to Sydney, they find only ruins. They return to their island and prosper there, essentially unaffected by the rest of the world or its destruction.

137. Drury, Allen. *The Promise of Joy.* Garden City, NY: Doubleday, 1975. 445 pp. LC 74-18774. Other Editions: Garden City, NY: Doubleday, 1975, 438 pp, [Book club edition]; New York: Avon, 1976, 501 pp, ISBN 0380005222.

This last book in Drury's series, which began in 1959 (see entries 88, 96, and 124), certainly deals with more cataclysmic events than did the earlier efforts. The opening is similar to *Come Niniveh, Come Tyre* (1973, entry 124), but the story is changed so that a conservative, Orrin Knox, becomes president. Knox inherits two brushfire wars, but they are reduced to insignificance when nuclear war breaks out between the Soviet Union and China. Knox attempts to mediate, but the warring nations fight on. In the face of apparent Chinese victory, Knox decides to intervene militarily, but the book ends without a description of how and with what results. Characteristically, Drury's conservatives are utterly good and his liberals totally bad. There is the usual superfluous background and dialog and the customary paucity of military details. This is another bloated Washington political novel.

138. O'Brien, Robert. *Z for Zachariah.* New York: Atheneum, 1975. 249 pp. LC 74-76736/AC. Other Editions: New York: Dell, 1977, ISBN 044099014; New York: Atheneum, 1981.

Competition for resources might be an important aspect of life after a future war, and survivors may be in the position of having to decide between human and material values. In this story, the only two known survivors of a nuclear war are a teenage girl in a rural valley and a man who wanders into her world wearing a radiation-proof suit. At first, the man is ill, and the girl nurses him. After he regains his health, he attempts to dominate her, at first psychologically, then sexually. The girl escapes, and for a time she lives nearby as they cooperate to farm and scavenge in a sort of armed truce. The man persists in trying to capture the girl and finally shoots and wounds her. When she recovers, she steals his protective suit and abandons the valley in search of a new place. Although both characters know that they might be the only surviving humans, they cannot live together. This moving story is expressed in remarkably clear prose in the form of a narrative by the female character. She emerges as a real and loving person, with kindness to handle her awful world.

139. Pangborn, Edgar. *Company of Glory*. New York: Pyramid, 1975. 174 pp. LC 74-10048.

The company presented in this novel is motley at best, led by an elderly storyteller and consisting of a half-blind boy, a whore, and a few jailbirds and wanderers. In 2040 A.D., 43 years after the Twenty Minute War of dim and imprecise memory, they flee the New England kingdom of Katskill into the wilds of Penn (Pennsylvania). The war has destroyed all of twentieth-century society, killed most of the population, and produced a number of freaks and mutants. There are a few physical relics of the Old Time, and life is hard but not impossible. People are ogranizing themselves according to medieval and frontier models. There is vitality and hope for the future. Pangborn creates this world with plausibility and consistency, and his characters clearly belong to their time. Some of the narrative occurs in the form of a diary that offers a second perspective at the expense of some continuity. In general, however, the book comes together as the ragtag company finds its way through a future that is neither too distant nor too dismal. Locale, style, and some aspects of characterization are similar to the author's *Judgement of Eve* (1966, entry 93).

140. Tofte, Arthur. *Walls within Walls*. Don Mills, ON: Harlequin, 1975. 190 pp. LC 77-358118.

Human mutation is the central issue for citizens of Resurrection City 70 years after the great nuclear war of 1999. The authoritarian government divides citizens into classes and controls their lives entirely. Mutants, especially, are sought out and destroyed at birth. Rolf, the mutant twin of a perfect brother, is hidden by his parents until he finds his way into the subterranean ruins of an old twentieth-century city and encounters other mutants. Rolf also discovers that the rulers of Resurrection City are themselves mutants who use surgically implanted electrodes to control the higher classes of citizens. When the mutants raid the city, Rolf and a girl escape to the countryside where they join humans and mutants living together in a frontier life similar to that of America in the mid-nineteenth century. This is an adolescent adventure story set in the future.

1976

141. Bova, Ben. *Millenium*. New York: Random House, 1976. 277 pp. LC 75-33785. Other Edition: New York: Ballantine, 1976, 295 pp.

Bova's excellent characters talk proudly yet desperately about their successful efforts to prevent war, but military clashes occur throughout. The plot deals with American and Soviet moon bases conspiring to declare the moon an independent nation at the turn of the twenty-first century. Population, ecological, and economic pressures have brought the nations of Earth to the edge of war. America and the Soviet Union destroy each other's ABM satellites, and troops clash in Antarctica. In a bid to ensure their own independence and impose world peace, the moon colonists attack and capture both Soviet and American space stations, and later they destroy a rocket carrying American troops on their way to recapture the stations. By threatening worldwide weather modification, the moon citizens manage to sustain their independence. The settings on the moon and Earth are described in thorough detail. The content of future science and technology is conveyed in a manner that is understandable to readers with a general education. Finally, the motive and ideals represented by the main characters are laudable.

142. Erdman, Paul. *The Crash of '79*. New York: Simon & Schuster, 1976. 350 pp. LC 76-22150. Other Editions: New York: Pocket Books, 1977, 428 pp, ISBN 0671812491; London: Sphere, 1982, 350 pp.

Erdman's novel of world financial collapse and Middle East war is remarkably prescient. Set in 1978 and 1979, the story's main emphasis is on Saudi Arabian political and financial manipulations. Their plan is to support the U.S. economy through guaranteed oil prices and financial deposits. In return, they obtain strong U.S. military support. The characters are rather thin, but the shape of international financial institutions and their arrangements are fascinating and seem accurate. Fighting begins when an apparant revolution in Saudi Arabia encourages the Shah of Iran to implement long standing plans to conquer the Persian Gulf. Iranian forces overwhelm the Iraqis near Khorramshahr and subsequently occupy Oman, Kuwait, and other small Gulf states. The war is a workout for the latest American military technology, although the Israelis are not involved in the fighting. In the end, six Iranian nuclear bombs are detonated which contaminate all Arabian oil fields for the next 25 years. Parallel to this is a worldwide financial collapse that devaluates most national currencies.

143. Harris, Leonard. *The Masada Plan*. New York: Crown, 1976. 314 pp. LC 76-22557. Other Edition: New York: Popular Library, 1978, 448 pp, ISBN 0445041897.

The nuclear suitcase bomb, a small weapon positioned at its site in advance, appears in a number of modern political and military adventure stories. Harris uses the idea effectively as his Israelis blackmail the world in July 1979. Several years of inflexible Israeli foreign policy isolate that nation while its Arab neighbors grow stronger. A massive and coordinated attack on all borders produces the immediate and genuine likelihood that the Arabs will push the Israelis into the sea. In these circumstances, the government of Israel secretly threatens to detonate nine nuclear bombs already hidden around the world unless the United States and other world powers pressure the Arabs to halt the invasion. Most of the action is set in New York, where an attractive female television reporter, a WASP businessman, and the U.S. Secretary of State work to defuse the crisis within a 24-hour deadline. After many adventures, they are successful. The Israeli blackmail ploy works. The nation of Israel survives, and the world is saved from nuclear war. This long novel reflects excellent literary craftsmanship. The story, in its context, is convincing, and the dialog is particularly realistic.

144. McGhee, Edward, and Moore, Robin. *The Chinese Ultimatum*. Los Angeles: Pinnacle Books, 1976. 338 pp. ISBN 0523009747.

In 1983, China and the Soviet Union go to war along the Amur and Ussuri Rivers in Manchuria. The battle lasts some days. Millions of men are involved using sophisticated conventional weapons. A re-armed Japan assists its Chinese ally with an amphibious landing on the Manchurian coast. The Asian war precipitates a European crisis that leads to the unification of Germany, the expulsion of American and Soviet troops from the territories of their former allies, and the destruction of Czechoslovakia and Poland. These events unfold from the perspective of the central character, an advisor to the U.S. president. No nation involved in the hostilities resorts to nuclear war, and without strong conventional forces, the U.S. is unable to exert leverage in the international situation. After the war in Manchuria grinds to a bloody standstill, the world sorts itself into new arrangements of power blocs, and the U.S. finds its influence limited to the Western Hemisphere. The writing in this collaborative work is smooth, and the presidential advisor at the center of the story is a well-drawn character.

145. Silverberg, Robert. *Shadrach in the Furnace.* Indianapolis, IN: Bobbs-Merrill, 1976. 245 pp. LC 75-31608.

In 2012, the world is ruled from Ulan Bator by Genghis II Mao IV Kahn. It is 18 years after the Virus War that killed two-thirds of the entire human population and infected the remainder and their offspring with organ rot. Shadrach Mordecai, an American black man, is the Khan's personal physician. He supervises the frequent organ transplants that keep the ancient ruler alive. Among his privileges in an otherwise decaying world is an antidote to organ rot that is in very limited supply. When Shadrach learns that the Khan intends to have his own personality and mind implanted in Shadrach's body, he performs an operation involving an implant that allows him a form of medical blackmail over the Khan. Shadrach uses his new power to obtain control of the public health of the world. He intends to enhance general distribution of the antidote to organ rot. Silverberg is an excellent stylist. Despite the gloomy setting, this is an enjoyable book.

146. Stanley, John. *World War III.* New York: Avon, 1976. 361 pp.

Several allegorical elements are mixed with such characters as a squad of chimpanzees in this unlikely but thoroughly entertaining account of a land war in China. No sense of the larger struggle or its origin is given. The time is the immediate future, and the combat is limited to conventional infantry action (plus the chimps). There is no indication of nuclear weapons. Among several notable characters is Sarge, the archetypical soldier who remembers or thinks he remembers serving in the Revolutionary and Civil Wars as well as previous world wars. There is also an earnest young private who wants to be a novelist, a wandering whore, and a few other standard war novel types. Their adventures in search of a treasure on a battlefield somewhere in China ends in death for many of them, but the war goes on.

147. Wilhelm, Kate. *Where Late the Sweet Birds Sang.* New York: Harper & Row, 1976. 251 pp. LC 75-6379. Other Editions: New York: Harper & Row, 1976, 213 pp (Book club edition); New York: Pocket Books, 1977, 207 pp.

The worldwide collapse that sets the scene here is the least competent aspect of the book. Several wars are fought, coups fail, people and animals become infertile, and a new ice age seems to have begun. These events are described briefly and without conviction. A wealthy extended family in Virginia survives because its leaders anticipate trouble and build facilities for cloning both animals and humans. Some generations after the collapse, the clones venture out, first to the ruins of Washington, DC, to scavenge scientific equipment. Separation from the group changes two of the clones who later produce an offspring, Mark. It is through this character that the central theme of individuality versus conformity is worked out. Mark grows into young manhood. He acquires the skills of a woodsman seemingly from nowhere and leads unimaginative clone foragers on trips to acquire replacements for deteriorating facilities in Virginia. Worsening conditions ultimately lead to the beginning of an authoritarian society among the clones, and Mark escapes, taking some promising children and fertile women along to found a new village. In an epilog, Mark returns to Virginia 20 years later to find only the ruins of the clone settlement. His own village is at a primitive technological level, but the people are happy, and each one is different.

1977

148. Asprin, Robert. *The Cold Cash War*. New York: St. Martin's, 1977. 170 pp. LC 76-62747. Other Edition: New York: Dell, 1978, 187 pp, ISBN 0440113644.

At some time in the future, probably the late 1980s, a Russo-Chinese War has occurred, and the communist world, called C-Block, has cut all communications with other countries. In the West, corporations hire mercenaries to fight wars against one another and against governments. The mercenaries use a type of armor that protects them from injury, and the war-making takes on the aspects of a rough game. Central characters are two mercenary soldiers, and considerable space is devoted to their training and other activities. At the end of the book, it develops that one of them is in the pay of C-Block, and he presents the West with an ultimatum from the communist countries to disband their armies in favor of an international force. The story is somewhat erratic and does not hang together well.

149. Duggan, Ervin S., and Wattenberg, Ben J. *Against All Enemies*. Garden City, NY: Doubleday, 1977. 456 pp. LC 73-22796. Other Edition: New York: Avon, 1979, 466 pp, ISBN 0380417235.

In view of events in El Salvador during 1982, the Bolivian War in this political thriller is especially interesting. An incumbent Democratic vice-president decides to challenge a sitting president for their party's nomination because of U.S. involvement in a war between Bolivia and Chile. The war itself is a limited, conventional affair with no more than 30,000 U.S. troops involved. In this country, it begins to inspire political and social divisions similar to Vietnam. The main character, a speechwriter to the president, urges the president to be strong and resolute and manages to guide him to a victory in the New Hampshire primary election. Characters throughout are rather vague, but the story is plausible and the settings, mostly in Washington, DC, appear accurate.

150. Goulart, Ron. *Crackpot*. Garden City, NY: Doubleday, 1977. 150 pp. LC 76-23764.

In 2015, the U.S. has broken into several independent states, although a shadow national government still exists. The Republic of Southern California is fighting a three-way war in Mexico. The other parties are the official Mexican government and the Mexx guerillas. The war and all civilian society are dominated by robots and androids that are made and controlled by a single giant corporation. The theme of artificiality is carried on relentlessly in this book. Crackpot, a reclusive genius, invents a gadget that allows its operator to override the programing of any nearby robot or android. After bizarre adventures, Crackpot eventually gains control of worldwide television to tell the world the truth about the war. There are many characters, all of them unusual, and continuity is not helped by an entire vocabulary of invented slang. While many of the ideas are original and engaging, they are often worked to death by endless repetition.

151. Ljoka, Dan. *Shelter*. New York: Manor Books, 1977. 224 pp. ISBN 0532124741.

In a depressing body of literature, this novel is one of the most extreme, probably because it is so effectively written. A global thermonuclear war is begun by China and immediately escalates with the detonation of Soviet suitcase bombs hidden in American cities. Fallout blankets the world and kills everyone except for the inhabitants of a shelter in Washington, DC, and other shelters in New Zealand. There are 20 women and one man in the American shelter, and Ljoka ably describes the degeneration of civilized behavior there. The New Zealand shelters hold mostly children, and mobs must be killed at the doors. Eventually it matters little because the radiation does not diminish, and those in the shelters have only extended their lives, not preserved them. The author's prediction that something small and slimy will crawl out of the sea again untold centuries in the future offers little comfort.

152. Rand, Peter. *The Time of the Emergency*. Garden City, NY: Doubleday, 1977. 151 pp. LC 77-75388.

Rand has substantial literary credentials, and Doubleday is certainly a first rank publisher. It is surprising, therefore, that this fragmented and confusing book would emerge from such sound antecedents. The story, so far as it can be understood, has to do with four persons living somewhere in the desert in the Samarkand Hotel. A recent catastrophe seems to have been a nuclear war, but that, like everything else, is never made clear. There is no central, continuous action; it is not really a story. Indeed, many sentences and paragraphs seem to stand alone, without relationship to one another. One character may be suffering from radiation sickness, but the reader does not know for sure. No doubt the writer sought to convey much meaning with this work, but it simply does not come across. Two careful readings offer little more than the experience of looking at all of the words twice.

1978

153. Anthony, Piers. *The Battle Circus*. New York: Avon Books, 1978. 537 pp. LC 77-91015 (compilation of the following three books: *Sos the Rope, Var the Stick,* and *Neq the Sword*). Other Editions: *Sos the Rope,* New York: Pyramid Books, 1968, 157 pp; London: Corgi, 1975, 172 pp. *Var the Stick*, London: Faber & Faber, 1972, 191 pp, LC 73-15533; London: Corgi, 1975, 172 pp. *Neq the Sword*, London: Corgi, 1975, 191 pp.

The idea that a society of atomic war survivors or their descendants might restrict the redevelopment of dangerous technology appears occasionally in future war literature. In this vision of the world a century after the Blast, the heirs of twentieth-century technology, called Crazies, survive underground and in secure shelters on the surface. They control a much larger population of nomadic warriors. Through their manipulation and distribution of food and vital supplies, the Crazies direct the Warriors into lives of ritualized combat with simple weapons, so that warlike tendencies are diffused. The situation is changed when a leader emerges among the Warriors who organizes them and leads a successful assault on an underground citadel. After much intervening action, the result of the battle seems to indicate that a synthesis will occur among the Warriors and the Crazies. Anthony's style is an unsettling combination of repetition and creativity. Countless long battles with swords, staffs, and clubs are described blow by blow; characters with very simple minds ponder and converse with compelling similarity about the meaning of life. In happy contrast, Anthony offers original and varied settings in several postholocaust societies in North America and Asia.

154. Bova, Ben. *Colony*. New York: Pocket Books, 1978. 470 pp. ISBN 06718196X.

Bova creates interesting characters, a plausible plot, and a consistent view of a future world in this long, competent novel. Set early in the twenty-first century, it deals with competition for control of a world with a huge population and diminishing resources. Among the organizations in the struggle are space and lunar colonies, international cartels, national governments, terrorist gangs, and a future world government. The main armed struggle in the book takes place in the United States with organized black revolutionaries set against army and national guard units that are finally victorious. The main characters are a young man from one of the colonies, a female Arab terrorist, and an English woman reporter. They have numerous adventures, and in the end, Bova presents a more optimistic vision of the future.

155. Hackett, John, et al. *The Third World War, August 1985*. New York: Macmillan, 1978. 368 pp. LC 78-25549. Other Editions: New York: Macmillan, 1978, 415 pp (Book club edition); New York: Berkeley, 1980, 509 pp, ISBN 0425044777. British Title: *The Third World War, A Future History*, London: Sidgwick & Jackson, 1978, 368 pp, LC 78-322077.

Although written as future history and classified by the Library of Congress as military science, this book is marginally a novel with imaginary characters and dialog. The authors are knowledgeable former NATO officers and officials; their command of background information and military detail is comprehensive. After preliminary moves in Yugoslavia and elsewhere, the Soviets launch a massive invasion of Western Europe in August 1985. Poison gas is used by both sides, and the Warsaw Pact superiority in men and armor provides initial gains. Within the first weeks, however, NATO forces are able to halt the invasion. Adept tactics, superior aircraft, and vastly more advanced electronics all assist the Western forces. Late in August, the Soviet Union attacks Birmingham, England, with a nuclear rocket, and the NATO countries respond by obliterating Minsk with submarine-launched missiles. The failed invasion combined with the threat of total nuclear war spells the end for the Soviet Union. Several Soviet republics rebel, and a coup brings moderates to power in the central government. After the war, the dominant world powers are the U.S. and the Sino-Japanese alliance.

156. Pape, Gordon, and Aspler, Tony. *Chain Reaction*. New York: Viking, 1978. 284 pp. LC 78-3528.

The war in this thriller occurs at the end of the book, as American forces leave for the invasion of Quebec. The story until then has to do with the attempts of a Montreal reporter, Taylor Redfern, to sort out a French-inspired plot to murder the premier of Quebec and replace him with a hard-line radical. The plot is successful, and the new premier declares Quebec's independence as soon as he takes office. The reporter, meanwhile, has been murdered for his trouble. Falling back on long-prepared plans, the United States uses economic coercion to force the government of Canada to accept an American invasion.

157. Sanders, Lawrence. *The Tangent Factor*. New York: G.P. Putnam's Sons, 1978. 308 pp. LC 77-21173.

Obri Anokye is president of Asante, a small country on the West coast of Africa, north of Togo. Asante is a former French colony, and the character of Anokye is modeled after Napoleon Bonaparte. With the help of Peter Tangent, an American oil executive, President Anokye plans and executes a successful military conquest of both Togo and Benin that requires only 12 hours to complete. Sanders is, of course, a popular and able novelist, and his characters and action are credible. He also has a sound knowledge of conventional weapons and infantry tactics, so the military portions of the book read well. Maps would help readers to understand the military action, but Sanders has avoided the obvious problems of illustrating relationships between an imaginary country and real ones. Anokye's dream is to unite all of Africa under his leadership, and his next target appears to be Nigeria. There is a question, however, whether he is really in control of events or serving only as the unwitting tool of the CIA. This is a quite readable novel from the author of several fine works, including *The Anderson Tapes*.

158. Topol, Allan. *The Fourth of July War*. New York: William Morrow, 1978. 311 pp. LC 78-15953.

During and after the 1973 oil embargo, many Americans believed that this country should seize Middle Eastern, especially Arabian, oilfields by force. This novel, set in 1983, works out the possibilities of that idea. Faced with a promised OPEC price increase of $75.00 a barrel, a U.S. energy czar collaborates with the chairman of the Joint Chiefs of Staff to take over Saudi Arabia with a military invasion. With the subtle aid of Israel, the plan is successful, and American troops capture the oilfields virtually intact. Military operations are limited to a single general chapter near the end of the book. At one point, Arabian troops, believing they are attacked by Israel, fire their weapons into the air and shout "Death to the Jews." The Shah of Iran is neutralized, and the Soviet Union is bought off with promises of cheap oil. When the U.S. president is once again able to control events, he orders the director of the CIA to kill all those who planned the invasion. In the end, most of them are dead, but the U.S. has an ensured supply of cheap oil, and the posturing of Middle Eastern personalities is at an end.

159. Turner, George. *Beloved Sun*. New York: Pocket Books, 1978. 371 pp.
The population of the Earth has been drastically reduced by induced plagues and a five-day war that occurred at the end of the twentieth century. It is now 2032 A.D. The survivors have established a world-wide organization called Security that controls the dissemination of all information. Security is also greatly interested in the protection of individual rights, and its policy is not to interfere in local government. These conditions prevail as the first interstellar flight returns after a voyage of 40 years. The story follows the flight commander's reaction to the world that is new to him and to clones made from his tissues taken before the flight. This person becomes the leader of a movement to change the world system, but in the end he is reduced to the status of an administrative puppet.

1979

160. Brady, Michael. *American Surrender*. New York: Delacorte Press, 1979. 292 pp. LC 79-391. Other Editions: New York: Dell, 1979, 366 pp; London: Michael Joseph, 1979, 287 pp, ISBN 0718117654; London: Sphere, 1980, 287 pp, ISBN 0722118449.

For most of its length, *American Surrender* reads like a modern spy novel. Through a variety of detailed and complicated means, the Soviets gain a measure of psychological control over the wife of the U.S. president. One of their most able female agents is the first lady's best friend. When the president, John Hurst, assumes office, Warsaw Pact forces launch a surprise attack against the NATO countries. By using an incapacitating but nonlethal gas, they manage to reduce the NATO forces' effectiveness. The Soviets maintain sufficient ambiguity in the situation so that the U.S. is hesitant to reply with nuclear weapons. Within five days, the Soviets are masters of Western Europe, and American troops, without their arms, are being evacuated from French ports. Then, by using their female agent, the Soviets gas the president and force his wife to go on national television with their ultimatum—the U.S. must surrender all nuclear forces within hours or face nuclear destruction which the Soviets have prepared. As the novel ends, the situation is critical, but the ultimatum has not expired.

161. Erwin, Alan R. *The Power Exchange*. Austin, TX: Texas Monthly Press, 1979. 261 pp. LC 79-66507.

In the early 1980s, the United States suffers from an economic decline and a significant energy shortage. The northern states blame Texas for exploitative energy prices and policies. Political schemes in both Texas and Washington, sponsored by OPEC secret agents, exacerbate a crisis that culminates with Texas' secession from the Union. As the presidents of Texas and the United States work with good will to resolve the situation, a renegade American general attempts an abortive invasion of Texas with the U.S. Third Armored Division. Despite this provocation, the two countries appear to be moving toward reconciliation as the book ends. The characters in this literate and well-researched work are complete, consistent and believable. The action is specific and detailed, and the essential premise is plausible. This is a competent novel, without the oppressive gore of many stories of future war.

162. Fane, Julian. *Revolution Island*. London: H. Hamilton & St. George's Press, 1979. 216 pp. LC 81-109172.

In this account, the narrator Adrian Michael Way describes the loss and rebirth of political liberty in Great Britain beginning at his birth in 1963 and ending in 2002. The country goes fully socialist in the 1980s to the extent that trade unionism leads to universal sloth and legal confiscation of most private property. This in turn is supplanted by a ruthless fascist, Sean Gwyn MacBull, who begins his political career in Northern Ireland by engineering the massacre of the Army of the Irish Republic and the subsequent surrender of the British Army. The British people, sick at the excesses of socialism, assist MacBull's rise to power. In just over 10 years, he institutes a wholly totalitarian state. Way is enslaved in a labor camp in Ireland. He escapes when MacBull's death brings about internecine fighting among this paramilitary units—the Bullyboys. At the end of the book, the Army has revived to assume control of Britain, and parliamentary democracy is being reestablished.

163. Macauley, Robie. *A Secret History of Time to Come*. New York: Knopf, 1979. 303 pp. LC 79-2087. Other Edition: New York: Knopf, 1979, 273 pp (Book club edition).

In the late twentieth century, a race war in the United States has expanded into a destructive worldwide conflagration. Hundreds of years later, all the blacks are gone, and the ancestors of the white survivors live in the fields and woodlands. They hunt and farm in a preindustrial society. Somewhere in what was Ohio or Indiana, villagers are captured by slavers from the South. One captive is the young daughter of an important tribal leader. The slavers are followed by men from her village and by a wandering healer. In the large slave settlement of New Mefis, the captives manage to escape with the help of their rescuers. The setting is quite pastoral, with much description of overgrown ruins of the "forefathers." Macauley writes dialog well, although his characters seem to have thoughts and conversations that are more sophisticated than their rude education would allow. His view of Southerners, at least those of the future, is not particularly charitable.

164. Palumbo, Dennis. *City Wars*. New York: Bantam, 1979. 152 pp.

Chicago is one of the few surviving cities in the twenty-first century. Most other cities and all rural life have been destroyed by the "levelings," a war among major cities that occurred after the national government broke down. When individual citizens of Chicago begin to be killed by small radiation cones, the government suspects that New York is the source of the attacks. A veteran of earlier wars is recalled to duty and is sent alone, across the wastelands, to reconnoiter New York. He finds that the citizens there are dead and that the attacks are the work of an unstoppable doomsday machine. His knowledge is, however, too late to save Chicago. The book ends with the immediate prospect of every thing being destroyed. There are subplots of revolution and romance in this short novel, but details are brief and action is condensed. The idea of cities going to war with each other is original and worthy of more complete exploration.

1980–1983

165. Abbey, Edward. *Good Times*. New York: Dutton, 1980. 242 pp. LC 80-12815.

About a decade after 1984, the United States has suffered a complete economic, political, and social collapse. A series of limited nuclear wars and the exploitation of the environment by big business and government have exhausted the people and destroyed national institutions. In Phoenix, Arizona, a few wanderers take on the local neo-fascist military government. The rebels include an old cowboy, an Indian, a few women, and a teenage boy. Abbey presents these outsiders as good, interesting, wise, noble, and heroic, while people who represent social structure of any sort are stupid and greedy. Abbey's informed eloquence about the rural Southwest ensures a beautiful setting, but the fate of humankind is not worked out at the end. The reader may wish that the rebels in the this story had the ability and determination of George Washington Hayduke and the rest of Abbey's earlier *Monkey Wrench Gang*.

166. Anvil, Christopher. *The Steel, the Mist and the Blazing Sun*. New York: Ace Books, 1980. 282 pp. ISBN 0441785700.

Two hundred years after a twentieth-century nuclear war, world technology has been rebuilt to an early twentieth-century level. Arakal, the warrior king of America, attacks Soviet-dominated Europe in a replay of World War II, complete with caricatures of European military leaders. Ultimately, the Soviets and Americans begin negotiations. From the discussions, it develops that the centuries-old global disaster may have been more a biological and botanical holocaust than a nuclear one. This disaster produced a Soviet spy and security agency to freeze technological development. It is this agency that Arakal and his army must overcome before they sail back to America. Despite its utter improbability and problems with characters and dialog, this is an engaging book.

167. Coetzee, J.M. *Waiting for the Barbarians*. London: Secker & Warburg, 1980. 156 pp. LC 81-136449. Other Edition: New York: Penguin, 1982.

An old soldier has served for 30 years in command of an outpost village of the Empire, protecting the border against the barbarians of the plains and mountains. Times and places are not identified. Soldiers are mounted on horseback and use bows and muskets. Other aspects of the story, particularly language and terminology, suggest a modern setting. The outpost is visited by aggressive troops from the Third Bureau who prosecute a campaign against the barbarians. The old soldier becomes infatuated with a barbarian woman and returns her to her people—an act that earns him imprisonment when he returns to the outpost. Like the barbarian prisoners, he is subjected to brutal physical and psychological torture at the hands of the Third Bureau. He ponders the reasons for this brutality and injustice but comes to no strong conclusion. A Third Bureau expedition against the barbarians fails, and ultimately it departs, leaving the old soldier and a few villagers in something like their original condition. Coetzee, a well-known South African writer, is able to ask questions about the role of a just and decent man in horrible times.

168. Gardner, John. *The Last Trump*. New York: McGraw-Hill, 1980. 225 pp. LC 80-16560.

This spy story is set in Britain in the early 1990s. With overwhelming conventional forces, the Soviet Union conquers all of continental Europe in two weeks. Russians are then invited into Britain by a depressed and infiltrated British government. Fadden, a British agent, is sent home by the American president to locate and activate ICBMs left behind by American forces. For most of the book, Fadden goes about his tasks in Soviet-occupied Britain. He and another agent find and activate the first missiles—armed with conventional explosives and aimed to strike barren areas in Siberia. This action is timed so that the American president can blackmail the Soviet premier into withdrawing forces from Western Europe. The agent is successful and Soviet domination is reversed.

169. Hoban, Russel. *Riddley Walker*. New York: Summit Books, 1980. 220 pp. LC 80-25859.

The most relentless and bothersome characteristic of this book is the phonetic spelling of the language of the future. Although its sounds and allusions are evocative and sometimes powerful, only a loyal or committed reader would bother to decipher virtually every line in the book. The effort is particularly disappointing when what is revealed is little more than a typical adolescent adventure story. Riddley Walker comes to formal social maturity in his primitive tribe at the age of 12. He lives in what was England, among farmers and hunters who know vaguely that they descend from survivors of a great war centuries earlier. Like most young adventurers in novels, Walker has a quest. He wanders across the depressing landscape of ruin to become unwittingly involved in the reinvention of gunpowder—an act that blows at least one experimenter to pieces. Shadows and fragments of the former twentieth-century civilization are everywhere, but if they come together at all, it is only to convey the vague and trite message that the human mind is a potent instrument for good or evil. The creation of an almost separate language, similar to English, in order to achieve a literary objective is a notable achievement, but in this case, the story it conveys is not worthy of the instrument or of the demands it makes on the reader.

170. MacDonald, Andrew. *The Turner Diaries*. Washington, DC: The National Alliance, 1980, © 1978. 211 pp. LC 80-82692.

MacDonald's vision of the future takes a particularly nasty turn not only because he imagines an ugly and warlike time, but because of the racism and religious bigotry in the book. In the 1990s, a central government run by Jews and blacks has disarmed free citizens through the Gun Raids and imposed other laws to destroy individual initiative and to elevate and enrich nonproductive members of American society. Turner and other old-fashioned patriots belong to a secret society that begins an insurrection in California. One feature of their revolutionary government is the forced evacuation of nonwhites to areas in the east still controlled by the central government. The civil war stretches on for some months before nuclear weapons are finally used. Israel and the Soviet Union become involved. The war is survivable although tens of millions perish. In the remnants of America, Turner's revolutionary organization is finally able to triumph over the government, and the racists and bigots are victorious worldwide.

171. MacLennan, Hugh. *Voices in Time*. New York: St. Martin's, 1980. 313 pp. LC 80-52916. Other Edition: Toronto, Canada: Macmillan of Canada, 1980, 313 pp, ISBN 0771595700.

The setting of this novel after a future war is almost incidental to the telling of a complex family history in the twentieth century. Around the year 2000, an old man in what was Montreal is approached by a younger man to explain some diaries that were found in the ruins. There have been several nuclear wars and at least three successive authoritarian postwar governments. These governments attempted to destroy or discredit all historical evidence of eras prior to their own. The old man, therefore, represents an important historical source. The family historian deals with one branch in Canada in the 1960s and 1970s and with another branch in World War II Germany. These family stories are well written, but the future postwar situation seems to be an awkward excuse for their telling. Moreover, MacLennan fails in an obvious attempt to bring the stories together.

172. McGhee, Edward. *The Last Caesar*. Los Angeles: Pinnacle Books, 1980. 304 pp.

The Last Caesar is not advertised as a sequel to the *Chinese Ultimatum* (1976, entry 144), but some institutions, minor characters, and supposed historical events continue from the earlier collaborative work. It is late in 1986. The American economy is in a shambles with both inflation and unemployment at critical levels. The world situation, however, is stable and peaceful. Nations are sorted into several major power blocs of approximately equal strength, and the threat of war is remote. A popular American president plans to impose radical centralized control on the economy. He intends to change the tax structure; introduce national rules for investment, wages, and profits; guarantee and require full employment; and halve the military. Before this program is implemented, leaders of the military-industrial complex stage a coup during which the president is murdered. A loyal officer assists the vice-president in assuming the presidency, outwitting the rebels, rallying the loyal populace, and saving the republic. At least it seems so at first, but the new president has ideas of his own about the future of the nation. Among noteworthy details is that men from business and the Navy lead the coup, and Army generals supply airborne troops. The Air Force and Marines are loyal. McGhee has an uneven knowledge of small arms and the sort of reader attracted to this otherwise competent political thriller might be expected to notice that.

173. Pohl, Frederick. *The Cool War*. New York: Ballantine, 1980. 278 pp. Other Editions: New York: Ballantine, 1981, 282 pp, LC 80-23589; New York: Ballantine, 1982, 288 pp, ISBN 0345301374.

The world of the near future is too energy-starved for a hot war because the Israelis have destroyed Middle Eastern oil with a nuclear attack. Horny Hake, a Unitarian minister, is recruited by the U.S. government to fight the cool war—spreading germs and economic chaos abroad. He serves with other individuals of unusual origins and personalities as members of a future spy network. Hake and his companions are funny, convincing, and interesting characters. They are moved by a powerful literary imagination through a future that is not utterly depressing. The features of this future world are revealed continually and steadily throughout the novel, so that the reader's attention and interest are regularly maintained and frequently refreshed.

174. Taylor, Charles D. *Show of Force*. New York: St. Martin's, 1980. 281 pp. LC 79-23125. Other Edition: New York: Charter, 1981, 346 pp, ISBN 0441761976.

This is a well-written and plausible story of a sea battle in the near future between American and Soviet fleets. In light of the Falklands War, which occurred after this novel was first published, the author makes accurate predictions about the outcome of modern naval warfare, especially the vulnerability of small ships to missile attacks, and offers interesting speculation about the power and weaknesses of battle fleets centered around large aircraft carriers. He also presents solid characters with consistent personalities and plausible dialog. The naval battle is confined to the Indian Ocean, and the participants are isolated from their higher commands because communications satellites have been destroyed. Commanders fight their fleets on the scene without much reference to higher authority, and other weapons available around the world are not employed. Although it describes a terrible slaughter, the book manages to achieve a positive attitude by making the point that the naval engagement did not lead to general world war.

175. Terman, Douglas. *Free Flight*. New York: Scribner's, 1980. 349 pp. LC 80-16635. Other Edition: New York: Pocket Books, 1981, 346 pp, ISBN 0671427350.

Characters are the particular strength of this story set in the mid-1980s. The United States is defeated by the Soviet Union in a brief nuclear war. Afterward, American collaborators establish a totalitarian regime in this country under Soviet tutelage. A pilot and a lawyer escape from confinement in a government facility and set out for the northwest in a powered glider. Like many novels about flight, the airplane is described in loving detail. After a running fight with government forces, the fugitives are forced down in southern Canada and ultimately die. In fact, most of the characters die or fail in the end, including collaborators who are presented with surprising sympathy and understanding. Subplots include a diarist's account of the Soviet decision to go to war that serves to set the scene and a romance between one of the fugitives and a Canadian woman. Neither digression is effective, but the main story of interesting men with different values trying to survive in a hard world is well worth reading.

1981

176. Ahern, Jerry. *The Survivalist*. Vol. 1, *Total War*. New York: Kensington, 1981. 218 pp. ISBN 0890837686.

At one level, this first volume in *The Survivalist* series is a survivalist's fantasy. A mercenary named John Thomas Rourke makes it through World War III because he is tough, smart, and well armed. His numerous personal weapons almost have the status of characters. To Ahern's credit, details of nomenclature and ballistics are accurate. At another level, this is an entirely plausible and coherent idea of how the current Afghan War might escalate into a worldwide nuclear holocaust. The Soviets initially have an advantage for three reasons. First of all, they have a workable particle-beam weapon. Second, they attack first. Finally, an indecisive American president lets much of his military force be destroyed on the ground before he commits suicide. At the end, Rourke is on his way from the remains of New Mexico to find his family in whatever may be left of Georgia. A few pages bound in from the next novel in the series suggest that there will be hazards along the way, but the Survivalist has made it so far, and he is a very determined man.

177. ———. *The Survivalist*. Vol. 2, *The Nightmare Begins*. New York: Kensington, 1981. 240 pp. ISBN 0890838100.

This second novel in the series is less interesting than the first because it emphasizes survivalist adventures rather than plot. John Thomas

Rourke and a companion attempt to travel across the Southwest toward Georgia. The Russians have occupied part of the country, and the remainder is in chaos. Rourke encounters looters, brigands, paramilitary organizations, Russian spies, and the remnants of the official U.S. government. At one point, he rescues the new U.S. president from Russian captors and returns him to free territory. After this improbable escapade, Rourke makes his way to his home in Georgia and discovers that his wife and children have escaped to the mountains. Again, weapons are described almost as fully as human characters.

178. ———. *The Survivalist*. Vol. 3, *The Quest*. New York: Zebra Books, 1981. 239 pp. ISBN 0890838518.

The high point of this third volume comes early in the book when John Rourke and a companion finally reach Rourke's hidden retreat in the Georgia mountains. Rourke takes the other man on a complete tour of the place, and its voluminous contents are cataloged in detail. Later, while still searching for his wife and children, Rourke is caught up in some resistance activities. He also acts as a private assassin for the Russian general commanding the United States and kills a KGB officer in a personal feud. By the end of the book, Rourke is less than a day behind his family and still searching fervently. As in the other novels, Rourke is almost a superman, the action is intense, and weapons are everywhere.

179. ———. *The Survivalist*. Vol. 4, *The Doomsayer*. New York: Zebra Books, 1981. 222 pp. ISBN 0890838933.

An element of scientific fantasy enters the life of John Thomas Rourke in the fourth and last book of *The Survivalist* series. As he combs the woods of Georgia searching for his wife and children, Rourke finds a geologist who tells him that the peninsula of Florida will separate from the U.S. mainland and sink because of the nuclear bombing during the recent war. To evacuate the population, Rourke arranges a truce between Russian forces occupying parts of the U.S., Cubans in Florida, and the official American government which is now called U.S. II. With much hand-to-hand and small arms combat, Rourke manages to save most of the population of Florida. His wife, meanwhile, abandons her horseback search for him long enough to lead a raid on a Russian prison to free some resistance fighters. Despite all this action, they still do not locate one another, and the Rourke family reunion is postponed.

180. Graham, David. *Down to a Sunless Sea.* New York: Simon & Schuster, 1981. 345 pp. LC 80-25603.

To the extent that any novel of future war can embody hope and inspiration, this one does. In the near future, energy and economic crises have turned the United States into a cold, starving wasteland where central authority barely maintains control. The first-person narrator is the pilot of a huge British aircraft that evacuates Americans to Britain where conditions are somewhat better. As the airplane is over the Atlantic Ocean, the pilot learns that worldwide nuclear war has broken out and that most of the major cities of the world are destroyed. In desperation, he lands the plane in the Azores at an intact American base whose personnel have been killed by a neutron bomb. Shortly afterwards, a Soviet plane, filled with passengers, also lands. These two groups of survivors establish that they are among the few humans remaining alive on the planet. They agree to fly to Antarctica where there is an American base with a small staff. Both planes make the flight successfully, and the people on board join with each other to plan a new and better world. This is a plausible, well-written book.

181. Haldeman, Joe. *Worlds.* New York: Viking, 1981. 262 pp. LC 80-51774. Other Edition: New York: Pocket Books, 1982, 239 pp, ISBN 0671435949.

In 2014, several asteroids and man-made satellites are in orbit around the Earth. They are called The Worlds, and their combined population of 500,000 persons supplies energy and some metals to the planet. Politically, The Worlds vary from independent states to outright colonies of Earth nations. Haldeman's heroine, a young woman born on one of The Worlds, visits Earth and finds it a fascinating place but plagued with too many people and too few resources. In the United States, an authoritarian government is opposed by a subversive organization called the Third Revolution. At the same time, a conflict emerges between The Worlds and the United States over economic and energy matters. These various pressures lead to war. Much of the Earth is devastated, and The Worlds are attacked. At the end, the planet is barely alive, and its remaining people have little hope while The Worlds, looking toward space, represent the best option for the future. This original and thoughtful novel is particularly readable; Haldeman is an excellent writer.

182. Ing, Dean. *Systemic Shock*. New York: Ace Books, 1981. 298 pp. ISBN 0441793819.

In 1996 the world goes to war. China and India are aligned against the United States and the Soviet Union. Terrifying biological weapons are used, as well as nuclear devices. Ing actually includes the war described by John Hackett in his *The Third World War, August 1985* (1978, entry 155) as a component of this novel. The United States, like most of the world, is devastated and diseased, but the central portion of the country survives under a Mormon president. Ted Quantrill, a former boy scout, becomes a soldier/spy for the new, streamlined United States and has various adventures. His character is less satisfying than the social, military, and political environment of the story, which is realistic and detailed.

183. Langley, Bob. *Warlords*. New York: William Morrow, 1981. 223 pp. LC 80-20572.

Langley writes very well. His characters are interesting; their dialog is natural. The scenes of action are tight and fast-paced. Moreover, he has an original idea for an imaginary war scenario. In the near future, England is close to economic collapse. North Sea oil has been exhausted, trade unionism has brought industry to a virtual halt, and commerce is almost moribund. The reader is led to believe that the American government sponsors a right wing revolution in England in order to ensure the political reliability of an old and important ally. The plotters are a crazy colonel and a handful of desperate mercenaries. Once fighting begins, the English government and military organize themselves to crush the rebellion. In the surprise ending, it is revealed that the abortive revolution was in fact a successful ploy by the British prime minister to rally the country. A minor shortcoming is that Langley does not describe handguns accurately. Otherwise, this is an excellent novel.

1982

184. Blumenfeld, Yorick. *Jenny*. Boston: Little, Brown, 1982. 90 pp. LC 82-083282.

The calligraphy in this handwritten book varies in quality with the mood of the fictional diarist, Jenny. She is an Englishwoman who experiences a nuclear war, survives in a commercial shelter for six months, and lives on afterwards in a countryside infected with radiation. Before the war, Jenny amused herself by buying clothes and cheating on her husband of 15 years. As Middle East tensions lead to war, she and her two children make it to the shelter, but her husband is locked out. For six months she waits with 22 other adults and 13 children, while outside radiation levels fall slowly. She occupies herself with self-pity and sex with various combinations of other people. When they finally emerge, the survivors find no people and few animals left, although they later encounter a gang of teenage marauders. When Jenny decides she can no longer stand to record her thoughts in the diary, there is no clear indication whether she will die or survive.

185. Da Cruz, Daniel. *The Ayes of Texas*. New York: Ballantine, 1982. 246 pp.

Enthusiasm, even love, for the pre-World War II battleship *Texas,* the state of Texas, and all people and things Texan is manifest on virtually every page of this imaginative but unlikely story. In the 1990s, the Soviet Union is more powerful than the United States and intends to impose a treaty that would further weaken this country. A Texas governor uses the vast resources of a Houston industrialist to modernize the *Texas* secretly and arm the ship with state-of-the-art weapons. Events assume their own momentum when a Soviet fleet pays an unwelcome visit to Houston. Texas secedes from the Union and Texan forces fight two bloody battles with the Soviets. In the end, the Texans are victorious; they maintain their national independence and motivate the American people to reject the unequal treaties. Characterization is generally unconvincing in this adventure story. The author's vision of future naval armament and tactics leaves out any role for submarines. Nonetheless, the book offers novel ideas in a competent style.

186. Hackett, John. *The Third World War: The Untold Story*. New York: Macmillan, 1982. 372 pp. LC 82-9879. Other Edition: London: Sidgwick & Jackson, 1982, 446 pp, ISBN 0283988630.

This companion volume to Hackett's earlier work, *The Third World War, August 1985* (1978, entry 155), is a retelling and expansion of the same story. More material is included about the Soviet perspective during the Third World War of August 1985, and there is even greater detail about weapons and condition of the military forces. While the first book emphasized the land battle in Europe, this one gives some attention to peripheral theaters of war, including Scandinavia, the Middle East, Africa, East Asia, and Central America. Hackett's ideas about political alignments and military moves in the last-mentioned area are apt in view of American involvement there in mid-1983. Hackett's books are barely novels, but they are fascinating reading. Together they amount to the most comprehensive account in the speculative literature about a future East-West war.

187. Harris, Brian. *World War III*. New York: Pocket Books, 1982. 240 pp. ISBN 0671442937.

Novelists frequently bring their future worlds to the brink of nuclear war, and such stories are normally outside the scope of this bibliography. In *World War III,* however, combat between small Soviet and American units occurs as the world moves toward war. In 1984, the Soviets send a small unit to capture a station on the Alaska pipeline. This action is in retaliation to an American grain embargo that has brought the Soviet Union near to starvation. A small Alaskan National Guard unit attacks and harasses the Soviet column as it moves toward the pumping station. Adverse weather isolates the action and keeps American reinforcements away. Meanwhile, American and Soviet leaders meet and negotiate in an attempt to stave off wider war. Largely because of the influence of hawkish Soviet leaders, the attempt is unsuccessful, and the bombers are launched to begin World War III, just as the small combat in Alaska comes to an end. Details of infantry fighting in the Arctic are unconvincing, but the idea of a small war ending as a larger one begins is tragic and successful.

188. Malamud, Bernard. *God's Grace*. New York: Farrar, Strauss & Giroux, 1982. 223 pp. LC 82-11880.

God is provided with a speaking part in this allegory of love and force in the immediate future. Calvin Cohn, a paleologist, survives a worldwide nuclear war while he is at sea in an exploration vessel. God explains to Cohn that he looked away while man destroyed himself. Cohn lands on an island that is populated by a growing number of speaking chimpanzees and a few other primates. Drawing in detail upon elements of Jewish culture that might not be familiar to all readers, Cohn attempts to guide the chimps into the development of a civilization according to his own values. He mates with a female beast and produces a living child of a new species. Despite Cohn's idealistic guidance, a few of the chimps have ideas of their own. They steal and kill the child, kidnap Cohn's ''wife'' and finally kill Cohn in a form of sacrifice. Malamud's great writing skill is obvious here. The clear message, that he might not have intended to convey, is that the future, like the present, belongs to the aggressive.

1983

189. Ahern, Jerry. *The Survivalist*. Vol. 5, *The Web*. New York: Zebra Books, 1983. 222 pp.

This most recent novel in *The Survivalist* series maintains the fast action and fascination with small arms that characterize the other four titles. John Thomas Rourke is still searching the Southeast for his wife and children who likewise are looking for him. By now, Rourke has quite a community of friends, both Russian and American. Mixed into this episode are hints of an American doomsday weapon that the Russians want very much. Rourke also finds a small town in the Kentucky hills where the few thousand citizens are determined to go on living a prewar life until they commit mass suicide. Rourke's favorite weapons are by now almost familiar friends to the reader. Nobody who reads all the books in the series can doubt that the hero and his guns will ultimately triumph.

190. Batchelor, John Calvin. *The Birth of the People's Republic of Antarctica*. New York: Dial Press, 1983. 401 pp. LC 82-22182.

Some readers may find that the undeniable richness of this work compensates for its tendency to be confusing and unsatisfying. Norse mythology is mixed with Christian religion, politics, and psychology to create a tale that must certainly be intended as an allegory of at least Western culture and perhaps the entire human condition. On the surface, this is Grim Fiddle's autobiography describing his life from his birth in Sweden in the 1970s to his end in Antarctica in the early twenty-first century. Grim and his companions leave the North in the 1990s because of plagues and an outbreak of Baltic wars. On their journey southward, they participate in a Falkland Islands conflict between Argentines and British colonists. Later wars in South Georgia and Antarctica involve an utterly bewildering array of pirates, refugees, international organizations, and governments. While these occur, there is only a general sense that events to the north are deteriorating and that wars and sickness ravage the world. Grim's thoughts about himself occupy many pages, and new characters and situations are introduced incessantly. At the end, the reader is aware of having read a very busy book without much sense of what is said or meant.

191. Prochnau, William. *Trinity's Child*. New York: G.P. Putnam's Sons, 1983. 400 pp. LC 83-4595.

This complex and interesting book suggests that a nuclear war could be stopped after a major exchange of weapons and the destruction of over one hundred million lives. Sometime in the late 1980s, the Soviet Union launches a surprise attack on American military targets. The U.S. president is temporarily incapacitated and, in his absence, U.S. military and civilian officials argue among themselves as they attempt to orchestrate either a limited or a complete U.S. retaliation. Programed war fighting orders in several computers and communication systems complicate the situation. Orders and counter-orders are exchanged, and the plot remains exciting until the last pages. Eventually, humanity prevails over the logic of destruction, and a surviving U.S. president agrees with the Russian premier to halt the war.

Author Index

Numbers refer to entries, not page numbers.

Title Index

Numbers refer to entries, not page numbers.